Lewis David

The 10-Day Alcohol Detox Plan

WinsPress.com
©2019

D1607781

Legal & Disclaimer

The information contained in this book is not designed to replace or take the place of any form of medicine or professional medical advice. The information contained in this book has been compiled from sources deemed reliable, and it is accurate to the best of the Author's knowledge; however, the Author cannot guarantee its accuracy and validity and cannot be held liable for any errors or omissions. Changes are periodically made to this book. You must consult your doctor or get professional medical advice before using any of the suggested remedies, techniques, or information in this book. Upon using the information contained in this book, you agree to hold harmless the Author from and against any damages, costs, and expenses, including any legal fees potentially resulting from the application of any of the information provided by this guide.

This disclaimer applies to any damages or injury caused by the use and application, whether directly or indirectly, of any advice or information presented, whether for breach of contract, tort, negligence, personal injury, criminal intent, or under any other cause of action. You agree to accept all risks of using the information presented inside this book. You need to consult a professional medical practitioner before embarking on any program or information in this book.

About the Author

Lewis David is an Addictions Therapist working in the public health system in England.

His work involves carrying out clinical assessments and working on recovery plans with clients. Thousands of drinkers have attended his therapeutic groups, workshops, and seminars. He has also trained treatment practitioners, police, and paramedics regarding alcohol issues.

By the Same Author

Alcohol and You

Change Your Life Today

The Emotional Mind

Mindfulness for Alcohol Recovery

For more information on these books, visit:
WinsPress.com

Contents

Preamble.

When you stop drinking, your body needs time to rid itself of every trace of alcohol and for you to become fully detoxed. The time varies from person to person. A lot depends on how much you were drinking before you stopped, whether you had been cutting down beforehand, and how well your body processes alcohol. But you should be fully detoxed after 10 days.

Those first 10 days are a tricky time for the newly sober person. As the level of alcohol in the body declines, you are likely to experience cravings, notably in the first three or four days. For most individuals, these cravings will be tolerable, but for heavy drinkers, these can be very unpleasant and accompanied by withdrawal symptoms.

However, if giving up alcohol was merely riding out some uncomfortable feelings for a few days, like getting over a minor illness, it would not be that difficult for most people to do, and you probably would not have bought this book. What many drinkers find harder to cope with is the mind-games that coming off alcohol produces. Things can get a little crazy.

Your thinking can become emotional and less reliable than usual. You will also come up against the power of ingrained habits that you have formed around drinking, especially if you have daily drinking rituals, like having a drink after work, or if your social life is based around drinking. Not surprisingly, many people don't make it through those first ten days.

But there is a simple solution. You are looking at it right now.

I have written this book to achieve two things:

Firstly, to walk you through those first ten days, making it as easy and painless as possible. Indeed, I hope you will find it enjoyable.

Secondly, to give you the knowledge you need to move forward and reach your non-drinking goal, whatever that might be for you. People will read this book for many reasons. You might be planning a short break from alcohol, like a 'Dry January'. You might want to give the booze a rest while you lose weight, get fitter, study for a qualification, or save money. A doctor may have advised you to quit because of a related health issue. Or maybe alcohol has caused you serious problems and you simply want to quit for good.

Whatever your long-term goal, you will need to get through those first 10 days and gain the skills to keep going thereafter. But you now have a plan to achieve this. It's a simple plan. You just need to read this book during those 10 days.

Yes, it really is that easy: just read this book and apply what you learn.

There is, however, a potential spanner that could be thrown into the works of this plan. Apparently, something like 60% of books are not read right through to the end. (We know this because, with digital books, the site you bought it from can track how many pages you read.) This is especially true of non-fiction books. I understand why this is. I've done it myself. You realize that the writer has said all the interesting stuff in the first 50 pages, you think "I've got this now," and go and buy another book or turn on Netflix or go shopping or whatever.

But this book is different. You need to read the whole thing and absorb its information so that the plan works. If you skim through the book and then put it away, you might retain one or two useful ideas, but it's far better that you

9

keep reading throughout the ten days because some concepts in this book will take a little time to fully sink in.

I've laid out the main body of this book to be read a day at a time. You will find that during those 10 days, we will cover much ground which I hope you will find thought-provoking and stimulating. You will learn more about yourself, not just in relation to alcohol, and the knowledge you gain will help you with other challenges in life beyond giving up drinking.

To keep you on board, I have done my best to bring in crucial new information right through to the end, and some of the most important material comes later in the book. Also, I will keep to the point so you don't read pages of waffle. I have gone over a few key points more than once, but this is to help re-program your subconscious mind, not pointless repetition.

So that's the deal: keep reading for the full 10 days.

You can approach this book in two ways:

You could simply start reading it as you give up, a day at a time. Alternatively, if you cannot wait to see what you're getting yourself into, you could read the whole thing before you stop drinking, then refer back to the daily sections while you give up. This would be more thorough and could also be a better option if you plan to cut down before quitting. (We'll talk about cutting down, rather than abruptly stopping, in a few pages.)

So why, you might ask, should you take any notice of me? Who am I to write a book like this?

The answer is that I have worked professionally with countless people giving up alcohol. My background is working as an addiction counsellor in the public health system in England. I carry out clinical assessments, one-to-one counselling, run therapeutic groups, and train other professionals in alcohol awareness.

I have spent many years at the sharp end of alcohol therapy. Some of my clients had only minor issues with alcohol and just needed a little advice and information to help them on their way. Others were hardened drinkers who needed medication as well as counselling support. And then there were many more in between these extremes.

One thing I found frustrating in my work was the lack of a good all-round book I could give to clients to read when they were not with me. I searched for such a book. I discovered that many former problem-drinkers had written well-intentioned books, but the research was suspect. Then there were many scholarly works, but they were aimed at professionals like me rather than my clients. You could say that these books were just too dry!

I decided that if the book I was looking for didn't exist, I would have to write it. So was born my first book *"Alcohol and You"*. I mention this now because I expect many people reading this book will have already read *"Alcohol and You"* and I want to assure them this is a very different work.

"Alcohol and You" explained the many options available to drinkers who want to reduce or quit, then left it up to the reader to choose the path that was right for them. However, I had many requests from readers wanting to know what would be my default way of dealing with alcohol.

This is that book.

Clearly, there will be some overlap between the two books, since they are on the same core subject. But they are complementary, not the same. If you just want to give up drinking, this book should be sufficient for you. If you want to dive deeper into the subject of alcohol treatment, then you might like to look at *"Alcohol and You"* as well.

I have tested everything you will read in this book in the real world. Through my face-to-face work with drinkers, I have had a wonderful opportunity to find out what really works for people wanting to quit. It's all very well for psychologists and therapists to theorize about what should work, but it's only when you talk with the people who test these strategies for real that you find out what works.

Free Audio Support.

To help ensure your success, we at WinsPress.com have created a series of podcasts: *The Alcohol Recovery Show*. I strongly advise you to use this free service as the podcasts will continue to support you long after you have finished this book.

To listen to the podcasts, simply go to:

winspress.com/podcast

The Alcohol Recovery Show can also be found on most major podcast platforms. To ensure you know when a new podcast is available, please join my email service at subscribepage.com/emailservice. (This is a confidential service. You can unsubscribe anytime, and your email address will not be given to anyone else.)

That's the preamble over. But before we get into the 10 days, we have vital preparation to consider in the next chapter.

Preparation and Tactics.

So now you know the plan: you need to read this book and absorb its messages as you go through the 10 days. Before you start the 10 days, however, you need to make two important decisions.

Firstly, what is your target? You might just want to do the 10 days. But for most people reading this book, the 10-day detox is just the start. So how far do you want to take this?

Having a clear time-scale in mind will work for most people. A break of a month has become popular. Dry January started in 2013 with 4,000 people. By 2018, this had grown to about 4,000,000 people. Other people will have longer time-scales in mind. Perhaps 3 months, maybe a year.

While time-related targets work for many people, they are not the only targets. Someone who quits alcohol as part of a weight-loss plan will focus on a certain target weight rather than a specific number of days or weeks without drinking. Or if you are reading this book because of a medical condition, your target might be to achieve a certain figure in a test result. So, if you want to stop drinking because of high blood pressure or cholesterol, for example, your target could be a test reading down in the normal range before you consider having a drink again.

Whatever target you choose, however, make sure that:

- It's a specific target. Having clarity in terms of where you are going is crucial. If you don't know where you are going, you could end up anywhere.

- You feel committed to achieving your target. If your commitment is flaky, your chances of success are much lower. If this is the case, you might be better to read through this book before you start your detox, as there is much information in the following pages which can help boost and clarify your commitment.

- You feel your target is achievable. So, for instance, if you want to stop for a month, but lack confidence you can do that, you could try just targeting the 10 days of the title of this book to start with. Then when you reach 10 days, you can target another 10 days with confidence knowing that you have already done it once, then another 10 days, and you will have achieved your month. In short, if your target looks too challenging, break it down into achievable chunks.

Many people reading this book will want to stop forever. But forever is a long time, and if you want to quit for good, I suggest breaking that down into manageable time-frames. It will help your brain to focus and increase your chances of success. You might want to target a month, which is a manageable amount of time for your head to deal with. Once you have done that, then three months will seem a reasonable target to go for next. After doing three months, a year won't seem at all scary. And so on.

In the chapters "Keeping the Score" and "Your Alcohol Audit", we'll look at easy ways you can use targets to power up your motivation, both in the short and long term.

The second major decision you need to make is how you approach detoxing your body. Are you going to jump right in and abruptly stop drinking? Or are you going to cut down first? It's essential you get this choice right, so let's look at the pros and cons.

Abruptly stopping drinking has a lot going for it. You just need to choose your start day and off you go. It's a clean break. If you are the kind of drinker who often has days off from drinking without feeling any ill effects, and you are not a heavy drinker, then this is likely to be the choice for you. Any other choice would over-complicate matters and I expect most people reading this book will go down this route.

If, however, you are a daily drinker, or if you only have days off drinking when you are so hungover you can't face a drink, then you might like to consider cutting down before you start the 10-day detox. This can work better for some people, especially if your daily intake is on the heavy side.

Reducing works best for drinkers who drink a regular amount because knowing how much you drink every day is a vital starting point. Your body will have become used to having that quantity of alcohol every day and it will have become a comfort level for you.

Some people find that they can suddenly stop drinking their usual quantity and carry on the next day as if nothing had happened. But we don't all process alcohol in the same way: your weight, gender, and genetics all make a difference. So, someone else drinking that same amount might find that their body and mind kick up a fuss.

If this is you, then you will probably feel shaky when you stop, you might have difficulty concentrating, and you will likely get massive cravings around the time when you

18

normally have your first drink. The cravings peak around the third day, so things will be uncomfortable and, as a result, your resolve might crack and you pick up a drink. At that point, it's game over, you've lost the detox game. Alcohol has won.

In this scenario, cutting down first is worth considering. A well-tried system exists for doing this. Let's take the example of someone who drinks a bottle of wine and two beers on most days. The idea would be to reduce in steps. Each step would be a reduction of no more than 25%. So, for instance, cutting out one beer would be a good start. You then stay at that level for about three days to let your body get used to having a reduced amount of alcohol in your system. Then you could cut out another beer, stay at that level for another three days, then cut out a glass of wine per day, and so on. You keep going until you are down to just a couple of glasses of wine per day, then stop altogether and do the 10-day detox.

The advantage is clear. If you have reduced significantly, taking that final step of stopping is much easier, you will have far fewer cravings, and are therefore much more likely to succeed in your plan. On the downside, however, some people find reduction plans difficult to stick to. Although a reduction plan might appear an easier option than stopping drinking suddenly, in fact, many people find the opposite. You need to decide which you think would work best for you.

I must add that there is one group of drinkers who should not stop abruptly. These are drinkers who have become physically dependent on alcohol. The reason is the risk of having an alcohol-related seizure if you suddenly stop. Seizures are unpleasant and can, in extreme cases, be life-threatening.

There is no shame in being dependent; it's surprisingly common. Research commissioned by the US government shows that 11% of the adult population could be dependent on alcohol at any one time. It isn't always obvious who dependent drinkers are because most hold down jobs, bring up families, and get on with life – their drinking is often when they are at home and goes unnoticed.

Signs of dependence include having trembling hands in the morning, waking up drenched in sweat, and having a drink during the day to get rid of feelings of withdrawal. If you are concerned, you can download a confidential self-assessment alcohol dependence questionnaire from me at subscribepage.com/alcohol-test.

If you think you might be dependent, contact your doctor who can make an appropriate referral, which may include having medication while you detox and read this book.

Other Habits

Before you begin, it's worthwhile considering if you habitually use anything else that could impact your alcohol detox. Do you drink coffee or smoke? It's common for people stopping drinking to be doing a general clean-up of their lives, and alcohol might not be the only substance they want to quit. While that is a worthy aspiration, I would be careful about stopping more than one thing at the same time.

The mind-altering effects of coffee are underestimated, so I would not advocate cutting down on that while you are detoxing off alcohol. You might have cravings you think are alcohol-related and end up picking up a drink, when in fact your body was asking you for caffeine.

Drinkers who are also smokers have double-trouble because the two substances make a very compelling mixture that's hard to give up. If you want to stop both, do one at a time and give yourself a long break between tackling each one. I would suggest dealing with drinking first because, for most smokers, drinking is a big trigger to smoke more. This is because alcohol causes nicotine to leave the bloodstream quicker, so the smoker needs to smoke more to keep the nicotine levels normal. However, it's less common for smoking to be a trigger to drink. So it makes sense to stop drinking first, as this will make quitting smoking easier in the long run.

Before you begin, I also recommend considering whether your detox is a commitment to stopping drinking or sobriety. They are not the same thing.

In my work counselling drinkers, I frequently find that my newly sober client will start thinking about taking another intoxicant to replace alcohol. This is understandable. If you are used to being intoxicated regularly, you have a period of change to go through during which you might feel there is something lacking in your body, and it's natural to think of ways to fill that gap.

With time, that gap will disappear, but in the short term, another substance might be appealing. In many parts of the world where this book is being read, marijuana is now legal and easy to buy, so it could be tempting to use this instead of alcohol, or indeed another drug. I would recommend not going down this route for several reasons.

Firstly, if you continue to get intoxicated, but with another substance, maybe the desire for intoxication is more of a problem for you than alcohol itself, and all you are doing is moving that desire to alter your mood to another substance. It might be better for you in the long term to look at why you regularly wish to change your mental state.

Secondly, if you take another substance, you are missing the chance to experience what sobriety can offer. Sobriety can be a comforting and fun place to be, especially if you haven't visited it for a while. If you are sceptical about that statement, bear with me and reserve judgement until you have read more.

Lastly, if you use a replacement substance, you could end up with a new problem that might be even more troublesome than drinking. For instance, I have known people substitute benzodiazepines (a group of legal pharmaceuticals that includes Valium) for alcohol, and end up with a nastier problem, as benzos are notoriously addictive and harder to detox off than alcohol as they hang around your system for much longer.

Having said all that, if you are already using alcohol and another substance like marijuana, when you give up the alcohol, you will have improved your health, even though you are still using something else. You will have made a big achievement. But be clear it isn't sobriety.

Audio

Before you begin your 10 days, I recommend you consider downloading the audiobook version of this book, which you can get free with an Audible trial. If you listen as well as read this book, you will find it easier to do your detox, as audio helps reprogram your subconscious mind effortlessly. To listen to a sample and get the audiobook, go to one of these links:

For the USA & Canada: tinyurl.com/detox-audio-usa

For the UK & Europe: tinyurl.com/detox-audio-gb

Timing

Once you have made your decision on whether to cut down first or go straight to quitting and taken any medical advice if that is appropriate in your case, there is one further choice you need to make: when do you begin?

Readers of my book *"Change Your Life Today"* will know that I am very much an advocate of getting on with it. Delay gives any doubts in your mind a chance to take root and undermine your motivation. Before you know it, you will be in a downward spiral of procrastination.

If you have a start date in mind, why have you chosen it? How far is it ahead? The farther away you are from your start date, the more chance that you will fail because you will find it hard to build momentum. You might not even begin. The way to get momentum on your side is to take action. Make a start before those negative thoughts can get a foothold.

In fact, why not start right now? This minute?

Are you ready to go to Day One?

Let's do it.

Day One.

Settling In.

So, Day One begins.

How are you feeling?

Quite likely, you will have varied emotions: maybe excitement that you're doing this, perhaps anxiety because you are already experiencing the loss of alcohol, maybe even resentment that you have to stop drinking at all. No doubt you will also expect this will be challenging, or you wouldn't be reading this book.

Whatever your thoughts and concerns today, I would like you to put them aside for a while. You don't need them right now. If you assume this will be difficult, it will be. If you expect you can do this, you can. Your mind will serve up whatever you believe to be true. So, rather than thinking of quitting drinking as a challenge, how about thinking of it as somewhere comfortable to settle into? Not convinced? Stay with me.

You have, I hope, a clear time-frame in mind for your new sobriety. That must be your choice: days, months or years, you own that time-frame. But as today is Day One, it's new, and just like being in any new surroundings, it can take a little while to settle in.

So today, I want you to think about settling into this new place we will call your sobriety. Start to check it out, have a good look around at your reality today and see if it seems different to yesterday, and if so, in what way?

Start to feel settling-in as being a physical sensation, a feeling of relief. You have probably experienced something like this in the past when you have moved home. In the run-up to moving you were busy, perhaps even frantic the night before the move with the last-minute packing, throwing those last items into boxes. Then the next day, you were off to your new home. It looked bare when you arrived, perhaps not quite the same as when you visited it with the agent, maybe you missed your old home fleetingly. Your boxes of belongings were all around you. You had lots to do. But for a moment, you paused and took stock of your new surroundings. You started to settle in. By the end of the day, you were getting sorted and the place was feeling like home.

I want you to capture that feeling and relate it to your new sobriety. It's time to settle in and get comfortable. And like a new home, your sobriety can be more than the place where you are now. It can become your refuge, your place of safety when your world is troublesome. In fact, rather than being the big challenge you were expecting, your sobriety can be a place of warmth and ease.

If you can feel this way, you will experience a mind shift. You will see that the conventional thinking most people have about sobriety is back-to-front. Most regular drinkers see alcohol as being that refuge. They see drinking as the solution to stress, loneliness, boredom, worry, a cure-all for everything bad in life. They don't make the mind shift because they never question that this is true. But these ideas don't stand up to scrutiny.

Let's take boredom, for example. I cannot count all the drinkers who have said to me they cannot stop drinking because they would get bored. But is alcohol really the solution to boredom? Try this test: imagine, you are in a room alone with nothing to do and nothing to stimulate your mind. You don't have your phone to swipe, you can't check your Facebook likes, you have nothing to read, an interesting view to look at, or a television to watch – nothing except a bottle of your favourite booze. So you drink it.

Are you still bored? Yes, because there is nothing mentally engaging or entertaining about alcohol in itself. It doesn't tell jokes, play games, make you a nice meal, sing to you or dance with you. It just sedates you. True, if you drank enough, it would sedate you to the point where you fell asleep, and that would get you away from the boredom. But when you woke up, still in that austere room, the boredom would be back immediately.

So, alcohol does not solve boredom at all. What alleviates boredom is a life full of interest and action, but you're less likely to achieve that if you are sedated much of the time. Sedation equals a lack of action, which leads to more boredom, so alcohol creates boredom rather than getting rid of it. It's like this:

- I'm bored.
- I'll have a drink to stop feeling bored.
- Because I'm sedated by alcohol, I do nothing new or interesting, so my life remains boring.
- Go back to 1 and start again.

So why do most people think that life without alcohol is boring? I think it's that most people drink, and therefore they buy into the narrative that sobriety is dull because they don't question it. But you can question that today. You can make that mind shift and see that, far from being boring, your sobriety is a place that can be exciting and much more fun and rewarding than your present reality.

Another great misunderstanding is that alcohol is relaxing. It is not. There is a difference between sedating and relaxing. Also, alcohol suppresses your natural self-control quickly, which is why drinkers often do and say things they regret afterwards. And their emotions take over, resulting in people becoming sad and aggressive after a few drinks. True, people can also feel happy when drinking, but it's an emotional lottery and moods can pivot while under the influence. You wouldn't call people on an emotional rollercoaster relaxed.

So you can make a mind shift now and see that, despite what most people blindly assume, alcohol isn't relaxing at all. In fact, it often leads to very unrelaxed behaviour, with sobbing or shouting. It's like this:

- I'm stressed.
- I'll have a drink to relax.
- Because of the alcohol, I get emotional instead of being relaxed.
- Go back to 1 and start again.

In your sober world, by contrast, you will find deep-in-your-bones relaxation, and we will discuss later in the book the easy ways that you can experience this.

As you make these mind shifts, you see that your sobriety is a desirable, happy, comforting and exciting place to be, a hideaway of warmth and safety that you can retreat to when life is demanding rather than reaching for a drink. If you are sober and relaxed, what's likely to go wrong in your life? Most likely not a lot. But if you are drunk and emotional, could things go wrong? Most definitely, yes.

If you are going through a testing time in life, your reflex action might be to reach for a drink because that's what you are conditioned you to do. But are you going to handle your crisis better drunk or sober? If I were a gambling man, my money would be on sober. So, if you can make that mind shift, and reach for sobriety rather than alcohol when life is challenging, you will understand that sobriety is indeed a safe haven for you.

So, as you go through Day One, I would like you to hold on to this thought that the true nature of sobriety is a nurturing place, and that by becoming sober today, you are going to be pampering your health and happiness. It certainly isn't gloom and doom.

Once you believe in the mind shifts, you will then be able to check in to your sober world any time you like. If you are intending to resume drinking after a break, your sober world will be there for you to revisit anytime you want to return – a place of comfort for you anytime you feel stressed or unhappy, a new resource in your life.

Nevertheless, alcohol will not leave your system without putting up a fight. Today and over the next few days, you will likely feel cravings, so next let's look at a simple and practical way to deal with that.

Easing Past Cravings.

I was running a discussion group once, when one of the regulars, Stan, was having his say. He was a sixty-year-old gardener who had a long history of being in and out of detox. I sometimes wondered why Stan attended as he seemed more interested in having an argument than a discussion. He had a talent for winding up others in the group.

On this particular morning, he wrapped up his daily 'world according to Stan' speech, saying, "I might drink too much, but at least I don't take drugs."

Stan had thrown out his bait to the group. Before I could intervene, several group members took the bait, and a bad-tempered exchange followed as people argued the case for alcohol being a drug, culminating in someone unwisely telling Stan that because he drank, he was a drug-user. The room fell silent as Stan stood up, red-faced with anger and eyes bulging. He announced, "I'm not listening to this rubbish," (or rather more colourful words to that effect!) and slammed the door on his way out.

I mention this little story to illustrate a point, which is that drinkers rarely think of alcohol as a drug and can get very

37

upset when someone points it out. Everyone knows that alcohol is an intoxicating substance, but many don't like to use the word *drug* because of its association with illicit substances. However, it's useful to understand that it is a drug so you can recognize what takes place in your body when you detox.

Although it's legal, alcohol is a powerful drug and, as the levels in your system drop, you will experience withdrawal and cravings. For many people, some anxiety and irritability will probably accompany these cravings, but they are manageable if you were not a heavy drinker in the first place or if you had cut down your consumption before you stopped. The important thing to understand is that nothing is going wrong – it's just what results when a drug leaves your system.

For heavy drinkers who have not reduced beforehand, however, these cravings can be severe and might even accompany physical symptoms like headaches, trembling, and occasionally even hallucinations or paranoia. I would repeat my warning to heavy drinkers not to stop abruptly. Cut down first and consider consulting your doctor in case your detox needs to have medical support.

For most drinkers, cravings peak after about 18-24 hours. So if you are the sort of drinker who usually has a drink at the end of the working day or before dinner, be aware that you will be especially vulnerable towards the end of Day One, as this peak period for cravings will probably coincide with the time when you habitually drink.

Therefore, I suggest you pre-plan what you will do at that time. Think about what is most likely to work for you. This could be anything from going to see an early showing of a movie with your family, settling down to watch a box set of a show you've been looking forward to seeing, or even just going to bed early – anything that gets you away from where you would normally have your drink, whether at home or in a bar. Cravings should drop off markedly after four or five days. However, with heavy drinkers, cravings could start building from as little as six hours after the last drink and extend to a peak after about 72 hours, declining towards the end of the 10 days.

So, what's the best way to handle cravings? To find out, I asked my clients because they are the ones who should know. In the therapeutic groups that I run for drinkers, I teach different techniques for dealing with cravings. It's helpful to have a trusted technique that you can fall back on when that mischievous voice in your head is trying to persuade you to give up this crazy idea of not drinking and go down to the bar instead. That voice can be very persuasive sometimes.

If you leave people to their own devices when they stop drinking, most often they will try to cope over the first few days through keeping busy. This seems to make sense: give yourself things to do rather than drink. It sounds simple enough. However, sooner or later, it usually fails. The reason is that people overdo it, get tired – which is in itself a big trigger for many people to drink – and they end up in the bar or the alcohol lane at the supermarket.

So, I carried out a survey among my clients, as they were well-versed in different techniques for staying off drink as a result of attending the groups and asked them which method had worked best for them. The answer they came up with was *urge surfing*. If that worked for my clients, it may well work for you too. So, let's find out what it's all about.

Urge surfing works like this: Start by visualizing the sea on a windy day. Imagine that the urge to have a drink is like a wave. It starts small, then gradually builds in size until it reaches its peak, then suddenly crashes and dies. It's important to know that the wave peaks just before the end.

So, if you are struggling with the urge to drink, remember that when the craving is at its strongest is the worst time to give up and buy a drink because the urge, like the wave, will be about to fade if you can just hold on a little longer. Imagine surfing that wave and you just need to keep your balance for another moment.

It's also crucial to realize that having a drink does not stop the cravings. Far from it. Having a drink just keeps the wind blowing and the surf rolling, so inevitably the waves (the cravings) keep crashing in. But if you ride out the urge, it's like the wind drops and the waves become less intense and frequent until they cease altogether. Eventually, there are no more cravings.

This imagery of cravings being like surf rolling in helps drinkers to understand what's going on. Having that knowledge is often enough to help people ride out the waves. But there are things you can do to help you stay on your surfboard if you need a little more support.

A useful idea is to focus on your breathing while you are riding the wave. Just observe the breaths going in and out. This in itself is calming. You can try counting the breaths to see how many you need before the wave crashes and the craving fades away. The great thing about observing your breaths is that it's so portable, you can do it anywhere when a craving hits you. It doesn't matter whether you're at work, watching television, or in bed. The breath is always there for you to call upon when you might need it.

If you have a few minutes to spare when you get a craving, another way to ride out the wave is to do something that is diverting and fun. For example, you could look up your favourite social media site on your phone. By the time you have got lost in Pinterest for a few minutes, you might have forgotten that you even had a craving. Which just goes to show that stopping drinking need not be hard work.

You might find it helps you to listen to an urge surfing recording. With this in mind, I have loaded an urge surfing mp3 onto my website for you to use. I suggest you download it on to your phone so you have it handy any time you feel cravings building up. All you have to do is listen. The narrator has a soft, Irish accent that will help calm you and take the sting out of your cravings.

The download is free to my readers. To get your copy, visit winspress.com, then click on the 'Free Stuff' tab, and you will find urge surfing in the drop-down links. You might also like to check out what else is there.

This is what of my clients said about urge surfing:

42

"I had learned many techniques for handling the urge to drink, but urge surfing was the one that worked for me. I think it was because it was so visual, it was easy to pull up the image of the wave in my mind. Whenever I felt that I was being pulled towards a drink, I would imagine the wave starting to get bigger. In the past at this point, I would start looking for a way to get a drink. But using urge surfing, I found I enjoyed watching the wave getting bigger because that meant it was getting closer to the point when it would crash and the urge would be gone.

Urge surfing rammed home two key points for me. Firstly, the wave would always crash, without fail, 100% of the time, if you just gave it time. Secondly, the only way to stop the waves was to keep riding them out. If you have a drink, the sea just gets rougher and the waves bigger."

Urge surfing is a great self-control technique to have in your locker. It's transferable to many situations, like binge eating and anger management, so you might have more uses for it.

That brings us to the end of Day One. We've discussed mind shifting, how common ideas about drinking and sobriety are back-to-front, and how sobriety is really a safe bolt-hole where you can settle in and relax, a place of comfort and ease. We have looked at cravings and how to deal with them.

On Day Two we get into some cool stuff to help you build on what you have achieved so far.

Day Two.

Thought Bombs.

Kelly had just arrived at the supermarket near her home to pick up some things for dinner when she found herself in the alcohol aisle. There was nothing unusual in that, as this was where she frequently shopped for her favourite wine, a bottle of Cabernet Sauvignon. The power of habit had taken her feet to the wine section. However, on this occasion, she knew she shouldn't be there.

After 10 years of regular drinking, Kelly was 8 days sober. Her partner, Martin, had raised concerns about the effects of drinking on her health. At first, she thought he was just being a bore and resented his interference. But she Googled research on drinking and was shocked to discover she drank far more than recommended limits. Although Martin had a beer occasionally, he was more interested in fitness. He was a runner and a regular at the gym. She recognized he cared about her and was thinking of her best interests. She announced she would take a month off alcohol. She wasn't sure what she would do afterwards. For now, she was just focused on the month. So far, she had found it surprisingly easy. The first day had been testing, but since then she hadn't thought about wine much. Until now.

She looked at the rows of wine bottles with their seductive labels and exotic names. She knew she should leave and turned towards the exit when she noticed a shelf of small, quarter-size bottles. They contained the equivalent of a large glass of wine. Normally, she would ignore these, as she would go straight for the full-sized bottles. But on this occasion, as she saw these, she heard a voice in her head say, "A little one would be okay. No one would know." She thought about this. Martin was away at a two-day training course in London. He wouldn't be back till tomorrow night. "You've been really good," the voice continued. "You deserve a little reward." Kelly watched as her hand reached out and picked up one of the small bottles. She took it home. An hour later, she was back at the supermarket, buying a full-sized bottle.

Kelly had been thought bombed.

Danny had been invited to a neighbour's midsummer garden party in the village where he lived. Around forty local people were enjoying the afternoon sunshine. They all knew each other. The atmosphere was relaxed. Danny was standing with a group of the local guys, chatting about sport. The others were drinking beer, but Danny had his usual drink: tomato juice with a dash of Worcester Sauce and ice. No one remarked on Danny's choice of drink. He had been sober since before he had moved to the village and none of his neighbours had ever seen him drink alcohol.

Danny was used to being the one who didn't drink and felt entirely comfortable with that. He had realized years earlier that he and alcohol were a bad combination. Sometimes he could drink with no consequences. But other times he would get drunk, and then his amiable personality would sour, and he would end up falling out with friends or family. Drinking for him was a gamble. After a particularly bad, alcohol-fuelled argument with his sister on one occasion, Danny had decided that enough was enough and he wouldn't drink again. That was six years earlier, and in that time, he hadn't touched alcohol. He had achieved that without getting help or going to support groups. He had simply made a choice. For him, drinking was a black and white thing: you either drank or you didn't. And he needed to be one of those that didn't.

Realizing his glass was empty, he went over to the bar, which was being run by a caterer who had been employed for the day. "Same again?" he said. "Please," said Danny, "A bit more Worcester Sauce this time." He looked away while his drink was prepared.

Danny knew something was wrong as soon as the drink touched his lips. Vodka. The caterer had made a mistake. He thought Danny was drinking a Bloody Mary. Danny went back to the bar to change his drink but had to wait as the caterer was busy with someone else. While he waited, a voice in his head suddenly said. "Don't worry. One won't hurt. You haven't had a drink in years. It's not like you have a problem with alcohol. It'll be fine." Danny drank the drink.

Each time he went back to the bar, the caterer said, "Same again?" Danny accepted and had another vodka and tomato juice. Two hours later Danny was stumbling around drunk, much to the amazement of the people of the village who had never expected to see him like that.

Danny had been thought bombed.

Thought bombs are very plausible, reassuring lies that pop into your head out of nowhere. They can happen any time, even to someone long-term sober like Danny, but when you have recently stopped drinking, you can expect to be thought bombed frequently. Common thought bombs include:

- Just one won't hurt.
- You can stop again tomorrow.

- You deserve it.
- No one will know.
- You can quit any time you like.
- It's not fair that you can't drink.
- The doctor is talking rubbish.
- You're funnier after a drink.
- This isn't a good time to stop.
- If you have one, you'll feel better.
- They'll think you're odd if you don't drink.
- You can switch to fruit juice later.
- A drink will calm you down.
- It'll be okay if you stick to beer.
- You don't have a problem, so why worry?
- You can stop next year.
- Better to put off quitting until after the holiday.
- Everyone else drinks so why not you?
- Those health reports are fake news.
- You're not as bad as some people.

Thought bombs try to persuade you that you can drink without consequences, that it's safe. But as Kelly and Danny found out, that's not true.

Guilt troubled Kelly that night. She had avoided Martin's calls in the evening because she knew he would tell from her voice that she had been drinking. She was awake most of the night wondering whether to tell him the next day. She hadn't even enjoyed the wine. It had robbed her of her peace of mind. She had gone from the nurturing and comforting world of sobriety to the stressful world of drinking.

When he sobered up, Danny was appalled by his drinking session at the garden party. He worried that he had destroyed his social standing in the eyes of the village. He was afraid that he could not stay sober and that alcohol would take over his life as it had done in the past. Like Kelly, he had lost his peace of mind to alcohol. He wanted to be back in the comfort and ease of sobriety but had doubts over whether he could pick up the pieces. This is typical of the damage done when a thought bomb explodes in your life.

So how do we diffuse thought bombs and prevent them from exploding?

Firstly, you need to recognize it for what it is. Thought bombs result from your subconscious throwing out ideas it thinks you believe, based on your past drinking behaviour. These ideas are enticing because they tell you lies you would like to hear. They tell you that you can drink without repercussions. You want to believe them. But deep down, you know they are wishful-thinking.

So when a thought bomb, like one in the list above, comes into your head, label it right away. Say to yourself, "That is a thought bomb." Be clear in your own mind that a deception is going on. Labelling is a simple and powerful way to defuse thought bombs because the label clearly exposes it for what it is. You can see that it's just a passing idea – and that takes away its explosive power. You realize it's not an instruction you have to follow.

Another way to deal with them is to consciously ignore them. You can say to yourself, "I know this is a thought bomb and I will not get suckered into believing it." Ignoring can be a good tactic, especially when you're busy. If a thought bomb hits you at work, it's not too difficult to ignore it and get on with your work. If you have a few minutes to take time out from your routine, you might try urge-surfing, as discussed in the last chapter, to diffuse it.

There are times, though, when thought bombs are hard to ignore. They are most dangerous when they arrive while you have the opportunity to drink. Opportunity is a trigger that has scuppered countless attempts at sobriety. Has this happened to you? Were you having a day when you hadn't intended to drink, but you noticed that you had the opportunity? A voice in your head said "Hey, why not?" and before you knew it, you were having a drink. If that's ever happened to you, then you have been thought bombed.

If you are at work or engaged in an activity that is meaningful and absorbing to you, then thought bombs are less likely to strike. But if you are at home with nothing to do, or if you are walking past a bar and you have time on your hands, you can almost guarantee a thought bomb will suddenly pop into your mind.

Some of my clients have had a lot of success with a strategy I call "Okay but not today", which is a great defusing technique. This is what you do:

Say to yourself, "Okay, I can have that drink, but just not today. I have to reach my goal first, then I can have that drink if I still want it." Say it with meaning. You can even imagine what you will drink and where, if you like, but it will not be today.

I think the reason this works for people is that saying, "Okay, I can have that drink," defuses the thought bomb as you are agreeing with its demand. If you keep trying to fight the thought, you might make things worse – you might get agitated and the bomb might go off. But by agreeing, you will probably feel more relaxed.

You must have noticed that if you want a drink, you feel more relaxed when you know you can get one. I believe that by saying "Okay, I can have that drink", you are recreating the same feeling as when you know you will have a drink. I expect that your brain releases a bit of its natural feel-good chemical, dopamine, which makes you feel better, so you relax and defuse the thought bomb. Whereas, if you want a drink but believe you can't have one or feel you're not allowed one, you feel more stressed, which is a trigger to drink.

When you continue and say, "But just not today," you are creating a reasonable-sounding condition. You are still not fighting; you are explaining to your subconscious mind what you want. This is essential because it's your subconscious that's throwing out these thought bombs, and it's only when it's convinced you mean what you say that it will stop.

By adding, "I have to reach my goal first," you explain to your subconscious that your sobriety goal is more important than the drink – which it is. This assumes that you have given yourself a clearly defined goal. Whether that's 10 days of sobriety, a month, or longer is not crucial. What is crucial is that you understand what the goal is and that you're committed to it, come what may.

This also underlines why, as we discussed in an earlier chapter, I believe that drinkers who want to stop forever should also have shorter-term goals. It helps your brain if you break "forever" into manageable chunks of time. If Danny had used a target, perhaps he wouldn't have drunk that Bloody Mary. With someone long-term sober like him, he would have had a more ambitious target than 10 days. Perhaps he would have an annual target. For long-term abstainers, using their sobriety birthday (the anniversary of their last drink) seems a clear, logical, and motivating benchmark to aim for.

I know some ex-drinkers talk about just doing a day at a time, and for people who have been drinking heavily for a long time, it might have to be that way in the early days, as they are vulnerable and have to keep the target short. But once you have a decent period of sobriety under your belt, why not extend the time to something more befitting your achievement? In terms of motivational psychology, it makes sense to raise the bar of your expectations – it gives you a sense of self-worth and forward momentum.

Day Three.

People, Places, Times, and Events.

Achieving most things in life comprises making a realistic plan and then carrying it out. Sounds easy, doesn't it? Make a plan, then do it. You can achieve just about anything if you do those two things. Yet, the reason we mess up in accomplishing our goals is that we fail to do one or the other.

The same is true for staying sober. So with this in mind, it's time to put a plan together for dealing with anything that might trip you up on your road to finishing those first ten days sober.

If you've ever looked into getting sober before – or giving up any addictive behaviour, like smoking or gambling – you will no doubt have heard of triggers. These are those things that suddenly put the idea into your head of doing what you're trying to stop. In my experience, triggers for drinking fall into four main categories:

- People
- Places
- Times

- Events

We'll look at these in turn, so you can see them coming when they crop up over the next few days. It would be helpful to write these down, so a notebook will be handy right now.

Starting with people, on a piece of paper, draw a line down the middle. Think about the people in your life that you drink with and write down their names in the left-hand column. Then in the right-hand column, write down any action you might need to take to handle your relationship with this person now you have stopped drinking.

With casual drinking acquaintances, people you only see in a bar, this is simple – just don't see them. Don't feel guilty. They'll survive without you. But if you have a more complex relationship with someone, let's say a person you drink with is also someone you work with, it's likely to be best to tell them what you are doing. You need not go into detail, you could just say you're taking a break from alcohol, so you won't be joining them for a drink after work for a while.

Don't assume you have to justify yourself. You're not doing anything wrong. You're not letting them down. You're doing something positive for yourself. If someone shows a genuine interest, you might like to give more detail on your decision.

60

You never know, the other person might think it's a good idea and want to join you in your plan. But if someone is negative or tries to persuade you into changing your mind, the chances are that they have alcohol issues, in which case the best thing to do is to keep your relationship professional. Don't argue. Just let them get on with thinking what they want to think. It's not your problem.

With family and close friends, be more open about what you're doing and why. Ideally, you want them on board with you. If they have seen you've been drinking too much recently, they might think it's a good idea and support you. But if they drink a lot themselves, they might feel threatened by having a sober person around, in which case you can put them at ease by saying something like "I'm just doing this for me, I don't expect you to change." Maybe you think they need to change their behaviour, but don't say this because if you are in any way confrontational with a drinker about their drinking, you can expect a defensive or even hostile response.

A good tactic is simply to ask for people's support. Tell friends and family your plan, say you want to detox and stay off alcohol for a specific period and say you'd really appreciate it if they could be supportive. If you ask people for help, rather than telling them what to do, they are more

61

likely to help because it makes them feel important and people like that. The more supporters you have on your side, the better.

I gave this advice to one client, and he took it to heart with great success. He lived in a small town and was well known for being a big drinker. Nobody minded. In fact, he was well-liked, as he was always amiable even when drunk. But it was sad to see him stumbling around the town. He had repeated attempts at stopping drinking but could never last more than three days.

However, something in our conversation about recruiting supporters struck a positive note with him and he threw himself into the idea. He turned it into a charity fundraiser. He loved dogs, so chose a local animal charity to support. He called his fundraiser the "50-Day No-Booze Challenge".

If you knew him, you would have known just how ambitious 50 days was for him. But it inspired him. He worked for the local council and asked workers there to support him, which they did. The animal charity helped publicize his fundraiser, and he even got some publicity in the local press. Everyone knew him and what a big deal it was for him, so his fundraiser was well-supported. Even his local pub contributed. The plan worked brilliantly. Everywhere he went, people stopped to ask how he was doing and urge him on. He sailed through the 50 days on a raft of good wishes and support.

With people who are not enthusiastic about helping you, it can be a good tactic to show that there is a benefit to them. For example, I had a client who used to drink with her husband. When she told him she was quitting, he was hostile. But then she pointed out that she could do the driving when they went out because she would be sober. In the past, they had always argued about who would have to stay sober to drive, so he liked that idea and warmed to her sobriety. That gave her the opportunity to ask him, as part of the deal, not to drink in front of her at home. He agreed, and they were both happy.

When you have finished writing your page for people, take a new page for places. On one side, write down places where you drink. On the other, what to do about them. With bars, the action you need to take will probably be to avoid them entirely. If the only reason you go to a place is to drink alcohol, what business have you being there if you want to stay sober?

Restaurants can be more problematic. You could consider going somewhere that doesn't sell alcohol. But if that isn't possible, try asking for help from the people you go with. For example, say there is a restaurant that your family loves to go to for Sunday lunch where you would normally have a drink. Before you go, remind the family that you are not drinking and ask them to help by not tempting you.

If you know it would be irresistible for you, then you need to accept that you cannot go. It may seem like a sacrifice but remember the benefits you are getting from not drinking. It's not really a sacrifice at all, your sobriety is a place of comfort and safety to relax in.

If your home is one of the drinking places on your list, you can't avoid going there, so you will need to decide whether to allow alcohol in the house. Some people who get sober don't mind having alcohol in their home, while for others, it would be fatal. This might mean asking other drinkers in the home not to drink there. Again, taking the route of asking for their help is likely to get a better response than demanding. But if that doesn't work, you need to insist rather than compromise and end up breaking your sobriety.

On your next sheet of paper, list times when you usually drink. For example, you might always have a drink when you get home from work, or you might always go down the local bar on a Saturday evening. Having identified all your drinking times, in the other column write down an activity you could schedule instead. Use your imagination and think of things that would work for you – but don't complicate it. Something simple is more likely to get done. It could be as uncomplicated as scheduling a walk with your kids or doing some shopping.

It's worth considering taking up a new creative project that you can access regularly at such times. Just throwing out an idea, for example, you could start or join a Facebook group for your neighbourhood, then instead of coming home and pouring a drink, you log on and see who's saying what. It might get to be so absorbing that you forget about the drink, anyway. (We'll be going into this strategy in more depth in the chapter "Your Map".)

Finally, on your last sheet of paper, list events you associate with drinking. For instance, you might watch football games at the local watering hole with your friends, or always drink when you go to music events. Try planning what to do when these events come up. Is it realistic that you could still go and not drink alcohol? If not, what will you do instead?

Now, have a look across your lists. You will no doubt see a lot of overlaps, like when a person is involved at a location and at a time as well. These overlapping items are your major triggers and the occasions when thought bombs are certain to hit you.

Such as, you might have a drink:

- with your partner (person)
- before dinner (event)
- every night (time)
- at home (place).

Or you might always get intoxicated on:

- a Sunday afternoon (time),
- watching football (event)
- with your brother (person)
- at the local pub (place).

Or maybe you always go out for a drink:

- at the local wine bar (place)
- after work (time)
- with the women from the office (people)
- when anyone has a birthday (event).

You have now identified your triggers, the time when you usually drink, and you have identified actions that you can do instead. Well done, you have a detailed plan. Now all you have to do is take the action you have pre-decided every time one of these triggers occurs. Remember what we said at the start of this chapter. You can achieve almost anything in life by making a plan and then acting on it. But if you make a plan and take no action, all you are left with is scribble on a piece of paper. So take that action now.

Relaxation on Demand.

I mentioned in an earlier chapter that one of the common misunderstandings about alcohol is that it's relaxing. You can see why this myth has come about, and few people ever question it. We hear from an early age that alcohol is relaxing, so we grow up believing that's true. As children, we heard it when we listened to the adults chatting, we heard it being said on television programs, and we heard it in ads for alcohol, which usually show people drinking in relaxed settings.

However, alcohol is sedating. It slowly knocks you out, which is a different thing from being relaxed. And the reason people generally look relaxed when they are drinking is that they are relaxing anyway. So, if you are talking to a friend about a common interest, such as a sport or a favourite TV show, you will probably feel at ease whether you are on a break at work with a cup of coffee in your hand, or whether you are down the local holding a beer or glass of wine.

It is the context that is relaxing, not what you are drinking.

So naturally, people look at ease when you see them in the local bar or pub as they have gone there intending to relax. However, there is a sting in the tail of drinking to unwind. As well as sedating you, alcohol also suppresses your self-control, which is why people often do and say things they regret after a drink. This also allows underlying emotions to rise to take over. So someone who is feeling in a low mood might initially get a lift from a drink as that feeling of sedation in a small dose can be a relief. But when any more is drunk, the low mood takes over, and the person ends up in a sorrowful mess of tears and self-pity. Or someone who has underlying anger might at first feel more tranquil under the sedating effect of the initial few sips of alcohol, but after a few more drinks, the anger takes over and arguments or even violence can follow.

Following this line of thinking, if alcohol actually results in people not being relaxed, then surely if you stop drinking, that will help you unwind, right?

Well, yes and no. In the longer term, yes – being without alcohol will help you feel more at ease. When you have settled into your sobriety and have found it to be the place of comfort and safety we discussed previously, then being alcohol-free can indeed be relaxing in itself. The peace of mind that comes from not worrying about alcohol-related issues will put you at ease. But in the short term, people can get agitated when they first quit drinking. You might have experienced it as you have been doing your detox. So why is this?

If you have been drinking regularly, and especially if your consumption has been on the heavy side, alcohol will have slowed down your brain's functioning. To compensate for this, your body will have been working harder to keep your brain firing up as it should. Imagine that your brain is like a bicycle wheel that needs to keep turning at a certain speed. Alcohol acts like the brake is being squeezed, so to compensate – you spin the wheel harder to keep up the speed. When you then stop drinking, it's like you suddenly release the brake, but you keep spinning the wheel just as hard, so the wheel is turning too fast.

This causes the phenomenon we commonly call withdrawal, and that leads to those uncomfortable feelings in the first few days. If you weren't a heavy drinker, the effects will be minor, because the speed your wheel (your brain) was working at while you were drinking wasn't too much different to when you stopped. But a heavy drinker will feel more uncomfortable because the speed will be more out of the normal range for a while until things slow down. It's also why some heavy drinkers need medication to help them

71

detox to slow that spinning down before it gets totally out of control.

However, now that you have taken the step of starting your period of sobriety, you can turn all this to your advantage. You can experience real deep-down relaxation like you haven't enjoyed before.

We will investigate in this chapter how you can call up relaxation on demand. I believe this is an important skill to have at your disposal when you stop drinking. When I have taught this to people in therapy groups, the feedback is always positive – it really helps.

Stress, without doubt, is a major trigger for drinking because of the belief that alcohol helps us relax. You now know the narrative of the relaxing effect of alcohol isn't true. However, although you understand this intellectually from reading the previous paragraphs, you will still have the reflex to drink when you feel stressed. If you have been drinking when stressed for years, this reflex will be tricky to overcome – it's an ingrained habit, a neural pathway you have walked numerous times. Habits like this remain difficult to control even when you understand they aren't serving you anymore.

So now we will bring into play a new behaviour that, if you use it frequently, can gradually replace that old habit with a new healthy one that will benefit your life. It's a way you can de-stress anytime you like. If you have previously studied relaxation techniques, you might find the rest of this chapter easy, but do it anyway. If you have never tried relaxing without a drink, you might find this challenging at first, but that's all the more reason to learn it.

To do this, you will need a few minutes when you won't be disturbed and somewhere comfortable to sit or lie down: an armchair, couch or bed. If you need to be somewhere later, it's a good idea to set an alarm because you might fall asleep. If you fall asleep, that's okay. Unlike meditation, where you want to stay alert, the point of this exercise is to find some blissful relaxation, so it's no drama if you nod off. Consequently, you can use this technique at night if you are having difficulty sleeping, which sometimes happens when you are detoxing.

It's usually a good idea to close your eyes, so read through the exercise once or twice to get the sequence in your head before you try it.

To begin, feel like you are sinking into the chair or bed you are on. Let your body feel loose and heavy. Let your shoulders sag, as we often store tension around the neck and shoulders. Let your body go as loose as you can. Then let it go even looser still and let those shoulders sag even more.

Next, slowly scan the areas of your body that are in contact with the surface below you. If you are sitting with your feet on the ground, you can start with the soles of your feet, or if you are lying down, start with the back of your ankles. Feel them melting into the surface below. Then gradually move your attention up through your body, feeling every part of your body melting into the surface below. Take your time. If you are stressed, you will want to rush it. But that's all the more reason to take your time. With practice, you will want to take your time so you can enjoy it.

When you are ready, use your hearing to tune in to the world around you. What do you hear? There could be traffic, voices outside in the street, wind in the trees, birds, rain on the windows, the hum of domestic appliances, or clocks ticking. You need not think about what you hear; it's enough to observe. If cars are passing, notice how their sound changes pitch and volume as they pass. Which is the loudest sound you can hear and which is the quietest? Which is the nearest and which is the farthest away? The number of sounds in your world might surprise you. Sound is always there. Even late at night, there is still sound if you are observant.

If your mind wanders off and you find yourself thinking about something or other, that's okay. When you realize your attention has drifted, tune back into sounds. If it's your first time doing this, a minute or two of observing sounds might be enough. If you do this regularly, you might enjoy taking several minutes. It's up to you. There's no right or wrong.

Next, when you feel ready, turn your attention away from the outside world to the sounds inside your body. There might be random noises from your stomach. You might detect a slight buzz in your head caused by the blood flow in your ears. But mostly I want you to focus on your breathing. If you have done the above, you should already feel pretty relaxed, so your breathing should be slow and rhythmical.

Ideally, you should be breathing deeply into your diaphragm. To check this is happening, place your hand on your stomach. If you are breathing into your diaphragm, your hand will go up as you breathe in, then down as you breathe out. If this isn't happening, that means you are breathing shallowly into your chest – a sign of stress. If that's the case, try feeling as though you are breathing into your stomach, and you should feel your hand moving up and down with your breaths.

No doubt, you will find that your mind wanders again. That's normal. When you realize this has happened, just refocus on your breathing and start again. You might find that saying "in" and "out" on your breaths helps to keep your attention focused, or you could try counting your breaths.

Enjoy the experience of relaxed breathing for as long as you like. Then, when you feel ready, turn your attention back to the sounds outside your body, gradually open your eyes, and reconnect with your day. Welcome back.

If you are new to relaxation exercises, you probably find that you go through the sequence in two or three minutes, as there is a natural tendency to rush it if you are at all tense. But if you practise over the next few days during your detox, you should find that you naturally slow down. I think 10 minutes would be a good target to aim for, so set a timer, perhaps starting at 5 minutes and then adding an extra minute each day. But don't obsess about that. The idea is to help you de-stress, not add something new to stress about in your life.

You find that once you have got used to this sequence, you can use parts of it at any time. So, if you are feeling tense during your working day, you can use diaphragmatic breathing to help you unwind. You don't need to be lying on a couch; you could be sitting at your workstation in the office.

If you are going out for a walk, rather than take your troubles with you and ruminate on them (which never helps) you could focus on the sounds around you as you walk, which is much more pleasant and will help you relax. And you can use these techniques at any time when thoughts of drinking are troubling you.

Many of my clients have found that stopping drinking brings huge benefits they hadn't been expecting, especially in terms of learning new life skills that they can apply to all areas of their lives, not just managing their relationship with alcohol. Learning to access relaxation on demand is one such skill.

Day Four.

Your Map.

When you stop drinking, you give yourself a wonderful present: time.

Time is something that most of us want. Look at popular self-help books and you will see what I mean. You will find masses of time-management books for people desperate to create more time in the day. We go on diets, go to the gym, and fill ourselves with vitamins and the latest healthy fad foods, all so we can live longer, gaining time in our lives.

Yet anyone who drinks regularly can gift themselves this precious commodity simply by drinking less or stopping altogether. Ask yourself how much time you lose in the week because of mindless sedation that you often don't even really enjoy, assuming you can remember what happened at all. This isn't too much of a problem for light drinkers – the sort of people who drink a couple of beers or glasses of wine a week – but as you are reading this book, you are probably not a light drinker.

If you are a moderate drinker, you likely lose several hours a week because of pointless sedation. If you are a heavy drinker, you could lose several hours every day. That's a lot

81

of time you could spend doing something more useful or having more fun.

You would think newly sober people would welcome all this wonderful extra time with open arms. And some do. But for many, it creates a problem. They are simply not used to having this time. Because of their drinking, their lives have become smaller, and they struggle to know how to fill all this time, especially heavy drinkers who have suddenly got oodles of hours they aren't used to having.

As people get used to being sober, their lives become bigger, they do more, have wider interests, and the time is taken up with cool new stuff. They look back on their drinking days and wonder how they ever had all that time to waste, wedded to a bar stool. But in the short term, many people complain of boredom. We have already touched on this subject, and I hope you made the mind shift to understand that the solution to boredom is not being sedated; the solution is having a more interesting life. Moreover, drinking creates boredom because it shrinks your life and you forget how you enjoyed yourself without it.

Nevertheless, it's one thing to say live a more interesting life, but how do you go about it? What should you do?

I have the answer. You need a map. But not just any old map. This is a special one that will make staying sober not just tolerable but desirable.

MAP is an acronym. It stands for "Meaningfully Absorbing Project". *Meaningfully* because it must be something meaningful to you. It doesn't matter if it isn't meaningful to me or anyone else, but it must be meaningful to you. *Absorbing* because it needs to be something that when you get involved, hours can pass by before you look at the time.

Your MAP is something you can go to anytime the thought of drinking troubles you. And a good MAP will be far more than just having something to do. That's where the word project comes in. Some people tell me that when they think about having a drink, they will, for example, walk their dog. That's okay, nothing wrong with walking your dog, but it doesn't work as a MAP. It's not a project. It's not something you can do anytime. If it's midnight and you feel like a drink, but your furry friend is zonked out in his basket, exhausted from being walked all day every day since you started your detox, then your strategy will eventually fail because it's not an anytime activity.

Something else I often hear people say when they are giving up drinking is that they will distract themselves. This is also okay – it can work short-term – but it's not as good as a MAP. Distracting yourself by catching up on jobs around the house you need to do, for instance, can work for a while, but if what you are doing is not meaningful and absorbing for you, then you will get bored and your mind will return to thoughts of alcohol.

So let's look at some examples of MAPs that would work. Remember, the criteria for a MAP are:

- It must be meaningful for you personally.

- It must be something you can get very absorbed in.

- You must have a goal, so you can turn it into a project.

- It must be something you can access anytime you need it.

So, you need to look at the activities that could work as a MAP for you. Probably, you won't need to look far, as there will be subjects for a MAP in your life already. Let's look at some examples.

I have had many clients take up yoga. Imagine you have done some yoga in the past and enjoyed it, so it was meaningful to you, and at times you got really involved, so
84

you know it can absorb you. You have already ticked off two essentials to making it into a MAP. How about the project aspect? Well, if there was a posture that in the past was beyond you, such as maybe you never got the hang of a shoulder stand, then you could set achieving that as your goal. Or if there was a sequence of moves, such as there is in Ashtanga yoga, that you would like to master, then making that your goal would turn it into a project. Yoga would also pass the test of being accessible any time you needed it. You can practise it at home at any time. You can read up on the philosophy of yoga anytime. To make it sociable, you can join a group and maybe you might make yoga friends and go on retreats or even yoga vacations. There are hundreds of quality free videos you can view to help perfect your practice. It is very versatile as a MAP.

Is there a sport you have tried before that you could enjoy now you have time? Let's take golf as an example. Imagine you have enjoyed playing golf in the past. If you felt that golf could be meaningful and absorbing for you, then decide on a golfing goal to aim for while having a period of sobriety, so you can turn this into a project. So pick your goal. Let's say you decide that before you touch another drink, you will win a competition at your club. The main way of using golf is simply to go out and play. However, you cannot do that all the time. But if you're home, or the weather's bad, or it's

85

dark, you can still pursue this project by watching YouTube instructional videos, reading up on sports psychology on your e-reader, or researching online courses you want to play. Maybe you could even book yourself a golf break away somewhere with the money you'll save from not drinking. As golf is a sociable activity, it also gives you the chance to meet people in situations where alcohol isn't the focus. True, there is always the temptation of the clubhouse bar, but I've yet to see a sign in a clubhouse that says golfers must drink alcohol. What's more, you might have to go into the clubhouse to collect your trophy and your winnings when you win that competition.

You don't need to limit yourself to one MAP, either. You can have two or three to give yourself a choice of MAPs to enjoy while you're not drinking. Consider looking at education as a possible source of a MAP. If I were looking for a MAP for myself, something that is currently an interest for me is learning the Portuguese language. I already understand it to an intermediate level, and I enjoy getting into the nuances of the language and working out different ways I can say things – but I would like to get better still. So would it work as a MAP? Yes, I think so, it passes the test of being meaningful to me. It's something I find absorbing. I can turn it into a project if I decide to pass a test at a higher level than I've achieved in the past. It would be easy to access this

86

MAP through online instruction, watching Portuguese TV, reading up on new vocabulary, and practising with Portuguese speakers. Also, I will have done something that will be useful whenever I'm in Portugal.

You might think about artistic pleasures as a source of a MAP. Do you have a musical instrument in the house you have neglected that would be fun to pick up again? Or is there one you've never played that you'd love to try now that you're sober and have the time? Would you like to paint or write? Anything creative has endless possibilities as a MAP, as there are always new aspects to explore and new things to research.

How about travel? Would you like to travel more with the money you are saving from not drinking? You can't be travelling all the time, of course, but it works as a MAP because the research and planning can be as absorbing as the actual travelling itself.

You might like to turn your attention to advancing your career or increasing your income. This could draw together several mini-MAPs, or individual areas of study, as you might need to learn new skills to improve your prospects. Have you had a business idea in the back of your mind for years that you have done nothing with? Now is the ideal time to give it some attention.

So what can you use as a MAP (or multiple MAPs) while you are getting into sobriety? I have suggested a few ideas, but the possibilities are boundless. If years of drinking have eroded your imagination and sparkiness, try doing a brainstorm on paper now. Ask yourself questions like these:

- Are there things you do that you have been meaning to do more of?
- Are there people in your life you could spend more time with?
- Is there something you used to enjoy that's fallen off the edge of your life because you haven't had the time?
- Is there something you have always intended to do but never quite got round to doing?
- Is there something you would like to know more about?
- Do you want to widen your circle of friends?
- Is there somewhere you have always wanted to visit but never got round to?
- Do you want to learn a new skill?

Write down all the things that might make a good MAP for you. Fill your page. Then put a circle around the ones that appeal to you most. Have a good look at them. Put a score out of ten next to each one for how much you would like to do each one. It should by now be obvious which one or ones to pursue. Next, just get on with one, start when you have finished doing your reading of this book for today. The best time to start anything is usually today. I believe that so much I wrote a book called "Change Your Life Today."

Earlier in this book, I promised that giving up alcohol need not be hard, and you can see that by using a MAP strategy, you are replacing drinking with something you enjoy. That helps take the strain out of giving up because rather than thinking about being without something, you are enriching your life and making it more interesting. You will also have time to devote to your MAPs because drinking takes up a lot of time. By quitting drinking, you will give yourself all the spare time in your life to devote to things meaningful to you, all those things that in the past you said you'd like to do but don't have time for. Now you do. Whatever it is you've always wanted to do, now is your chance.

Your True Motivation.

Understanding your true motivation to cease drinking is vital if you are going to meet your long-term goal, whether you want to stop for a month or forever. Contrast these two reasons for stopping drinking:

Maria has been the same dress size since she was a teenager, but now in her early thirties, she struggles to fit into her favourite clothes and faces having to buy a size larger. This has coincided with an increase in her alcohol consumption. She has been in a new relationship for a few months with Lawrence, who likes a drink and has been taking her out several times per week. Maria enjoys this, and especially a few glasses of Chardonnay. But whereas she used to be a light drinker, consuming only about a bottle a week before meeting Lawrence, she has been keeping track of her drinking and has realized she is drinking about five bottles weekly now.

Lawrence doesn't care that she has put on weight. He says she looks good anyway. But Maria cares. She doesn't like what she sees in the mirror and hates not feeling comfortable when she dresses. Her clothes used to glide on, now she needs to push herself into them. It also concerns her that on the days when she doesn't drink, she misses it. That never used to happen.

Maria has done some research, and it startled her to discover that those extra bottles of wine she has been drinking amount to an extra 2,400 calories weekly. Given that an average woman needs just 2,000 calories per day, that means she is consuming more than an extra day's calories every week, just drinking wine with Lawrence. No wonder she has gone up a dress size.

Maria has decided to stop this now. Feeling comfortable in her clothes and consequently feeling good about herself is more important to her than alcohol. She has calculated that if she stops drinking completely and limits her calories to 1,500 per day, she will be back to her old weight in eight weeks. At that point, she might go back to having the occasional glass, but not to drinking five bottles weekly again. She has discussed this with Lawrence, who said he didn't want to stop drinking himself, but to support Maria, he wouldn't drink while he was with her during the eight weeks.

Will Maria succeed? Yes, I think she has everything in her favour. She has a clear plan and the support of Lawrence.

But I think the most important factor is that she is doing it for herself, not for Lawrence or anyone else, and not because she wants to look like anyone else – she just wants to be comfortable in her clothes again. It's a matter of self-respect and a positive self-image. If Lawrence hadn't supported her, it might have been more difficult, but she would have done it anyway.

Steven is in a different situation. He loves nothing more than meeting his friends after work and having some drinks and laughs. He has done this since he was a teenager. He considers it normal male behaviour. Then he met Ella, who quickly became pregnant, and Steven moved in with her. Steven tried to modify his behaviour during her pregnancy, and he spent more time with her, although he was sneaking drinks at home after she went to bed. Since the baby was born, he has been spending more and more time with his pals, getting home late and slobbing out on the couch.

Ella has had enough. She has made it plain that if he doesn't stop drinking, she will throw him out. This shocked Steven. He realizes that without Ella his life could fall apart. He says that he doesn't want to stop, but to keep her happy, he will start cutting back and eventually quit altogether.

So what are Steven's chances of success? Rather small, in my opinion. He doesn't want to stop. We know he regards his behaviour as normal, but he wants to keep Ella off his back and prevent bad things from happening in his life. He has no real plan. Even though the fear of breaking up with Ella might make him try to cut down and stop, and even if on a conscious level he believes he is trying, his subconscious mind will undermine him. His subconscious knows he really doesn't want to quit and will likely persuade him to cheat on the arrangement. He will probably start drinking in secret again, as he did while she was pregnant. In the end, he will wear Ella down, and she will either resentfully tolerate his drinking or she will throw him out. Not good outcomes for their family either way.

Having a positive desire to stop is crucial. If you don't have one, your subconscious mind will intervene, using its favourite weapon to undermine you: the thought bomb.

So why does your mind do this? I discovered the answer while I was investigating hypnosis as a way of dealing with excess drinking. It puzzled me that hypnosis was never used as a treatment for drinkers, since it has a respectable record of helping smokers quit. They are both addictive substances, so it made no sense that it would work with nicotine but not alcohol. Yet although I knew many people

94

who had quit smoking with hypnosis, I had never met one who had succeeded with drinking. Is this because nicotine is less addictive? No, not at all – nicotine is right up there at number one as the deadliest addictive substance the world has seen.

I discovered the answer from a successful hypnotherapist. He explained that hypnosis can cure a vast amount of problems, but one thing was always necessary: the person being hypnotised must want it to work. Without that desire, the subconscious will overcome hypnosis every time.

That made sense. Smokers usually want to quit. They are in no doubt that they are in the grip of a powerful addiction that quite likely will kill them. They don't really enjoy it. The only pleasure from smoking is in relieving the withdrawal, which starts almost as soon as they finish the last smoke. Also, smoking has become socially unacceptable, and many countries nowadays treat smokers like pariahs.

In contrast, drinkers don't have the same motivation, which is the problem. And poor motivation is likely to sabotage your efforts to stop drinking whatever method you use, whether it be hypnosis, willpower, meditation, going to groups, getting spiritual, or going to the gym. Even using anti-craving medications will ultimately fail if your motivation is negative.

Putting it bluntly, most drinkers who say they want to quit don't mean it. They might have talked themselves into thinking they do, but their subconscious knows the truth and will throw out thought bombs to blow up their plans for sobriety. So just as your subconscious will undermine hypnosis if you don't genuinely want it to work, it will sabotage other methods as well.

Therefore, look at your reasons to quit now. Get deep-down honest with yourself. What is your real reason for quitting? If it's something you are genuinely doing for yourself and you really want to quit, then you will find your reasons motivating. But it will be hard going if you are quitting for one of these two reasons:

- You don't want to quit, but you feel that you should quit. Negative publicity about the effects of alcohol might have swayed you, for example, but your heart isn't in it and you don't want to stop. Your subconscious knows your commitment is flaky and will be on the lookout for an excuse you can use to drink again, such as "Oh, I read somewhere on Facebook that red wine is high in antioxidants, so I thought I'd better start drinking again." You know it's just an excuse, and if you genuinely want more antioxidants, you would be far better eating a few blueberries than drinking wine. But it's a justification you can give to your family for why you gave up your plan to quit after just a few days.

- You are quitting because of pressure from someone else. Maybe like Steven, you have been under pressure from close family because of something you have done. Or perhaps alcohol has got you into trouble, such as a drink-driving offence, and the authorities are on your back. You are probably feeling hard-done-by and resentful and are busy blaming everyone apart from yourself for your behaviour that got you into this mess. Meanwhile, your subconscious will look for opportunities to get you out of it and start backsliding. My experience of working with drinkers who feel under pressure to stop is that it rarely has a good outcome for the individual concerned unless they make a mind shift. Instead of wasting your time nursing your resentments and cursing your luck, try looking for what you can get out of the situation. The smart thinker should look for a win-win situation, so the person applying the pressure is happy and stays off your back, and you feel you have come out with positives too.

If either of the above applies to you, it's time to do more mind shifting to build positive motivation and enthusiasm about quitting drinking rather than thinking it's just a huge chore.

You can do this by getting granular about your motivation. To do this, you just need a few minutes and something to write on. Write down the areas of life important to you. I leave it up to you to decide what those are, but here are some suggestions: family, health, relationships, money, career, social standing, legal, ambitions, qualifications, self-respect, hobbies, and vacations. Some of these might not apply to you. If you're retired, you won't prioritize a career unless you want a new one. If you're rolling in cash and light your cigars with hundred-dollar bills, you might leave money off your list. On the other hand, if you're studying for a diploma, for example, then qualifications would be close to the top of your list. Get busy for a few minutes and write down all the life categories you can think of that apply to you. Then look at what you've written and pick the four or five categories that are most important to you. We will work with these.

Next, write down for each category how quitting drinking will help. And get detailed, go granular. This is important because let's say you have money as one of your most important categories. You could write down, "I'll save money." But this is a kind of "So what?" statement. You know already that you'll save money – writing that down will not put a rocket under your motivation.

So go granular: work out exactly how much you spend on drinks (which might be scary and something you have been avoiding looking at) and work out where that money could be better spent, such as paying off your credit cards or upgrading your car. How many weeks would you need to stay off the booze to finance that and feel great about yourself?

If your target is more short-term – for instance, maybe you're having a month of sobriety while you read this book – work out exactly how much you will save and what you will do with the money. If you decide that you want to get those new shoes you've been admiring but think seem too expensive, put them down on your granular list and buy them at the end of your month.

Getting into detail like this, you should end up with a long list of the benefits of stopping drinking for you. It's your list for your life. You own it. Keep it and look at it regularly. Put it somewhere prominent. Maybe pin it up next to your PC or stick it to the fridge door – anywhere you will see it often.

This will do two things. Firstly, on a conscious level, it will build your motivation. Secondly, it will help to reprogram your subconscious mind to help you, because your subconscious will find it hard to ignore the benefits when there are so many written down in front of you.

Day Five.

Keeping the Score.

Especially in the early days of sobriety, keeping a track of how long you have been sober is motivating for most people. We should not underestimate the simple act of counting the days. In fact, I encourage clients I work with to do this in a very bold way, such as putting up a wall chart and crossing off the days with a marker pen. That might sound simplistic, even perhaps juvenile, but having worked with so many drinkers, I can say, without doubt, it works. Big, bold, and basic works much better than clever and sophisticated every time.

It's easy to see why. If you have, say, an app on your phone to track your days of sobriety, well, it's all too easy not to look at it. I mean, how many apps do you have on your phone? It's easy for one to get lost in the crowd. You pick up your phone to check your sobriety app, but you notice that you've got loads of messages coming in on WhatsApp, and before you know it, you've forgotten all about the little sobriety app. But if you have a huge sobriety wall chart that you can't miss every time you walk into your home, that not only reminds you, it also sends a big bold message to your subconscious: you're serious about this. So keep a track of your days in a big, vibrant way and be proud of what you've achieved.

Tracking days is not the only way you can use numbers to motivate you. If you are staying off alcohol to lose weight, then recording your weight every day, or tracking your Body Mass Index, will resonate with you more than your total of days sober. If you have a medical condition, then getting regular test readings will be more appropriate. But whatever method you choose, make sure you have a target and a way of tracking it visually.

It also helps to make your target public. Share it with your family and friends. This will, all being well, get them on board with your project and they can encourage you. But just as importantly, it makes it more difficult for you to backslide. Imagine, for instance, that you have bought this book because the title appealed to you, and you thought doing a 10-day detox sounded good. That's great. But if you buy this book, keep it on your e-reader and don't tell a soul, then when you have a bad day it makes it easy to pick up a drink because no one will know.

On the other hand, if you've told everyone on your Instagram account that you are doing this detox, put up a wall chart where all your family can see it, and made a hundred-dollar bet with all your drinking buddies that you can do this, you would be less likely to backslide because of the risk of embarrassment – and you wanted to take that money off your buddies. You have more invested in your success.

However, I have some reservations with target-setting that, in the interests of completeness, I need to share with you so that you don't get caught out. The first is where drinkers set a short-term goal like a month, which has become a popular, even fashionable thing to do in the last few years. Giving your body a rest from alcohol would seem to make total sense. Where the problem lies is with people who use the month as an excuse to go out bingeing afterwards. They feel they have "done their time", so to speak. They feel they have credit in the bank of good health, and this gives them licence to drink like a drain in a flash flood when the month is over. But the reality is different.

After a month off the booze, you might feel much better and think you have made reparations for the last year of drinking. However, your body will need more than a month to right itself, especially if you are usually a heavy drinker. Your brain alone could need as much as a year to recover fully. We know this because researchers have discovered that the size of the brains of heavy drinkers are smaller than

105

they should be, and it takes up to 12 months of abstinence from alcohol for the brain to regain normal size. So after a month, your body is still in the early stages of recovery. Going out and bingeing because you have just done 31 days will quickly put your mind and body back to square one. You haven't got the credit in the bank of good health that you thought you had. You've deluded yourself.

So if you are reading this book to support you through a Dry January, or any other month or short period away from alcohol, I would like to offer you two thoughts to consider. Think about making your month the start of the journey rather than the entire voyage. Once you've done your month, could you maybe do another one and give your mind and body more time to get well? Or if you return to drinking, how about taking it easy rather than going at it like a parched horse? (In the chapter "Your Alcohol Audit" we will look at a way of monitoring where you are in health terms over longer periods of time with your drinking.)

I would also like to address readers who have in mind the target of long-term sobriety. Most often, these are people who have had bad things happen in their lives and have realized that alcohol was to blame. The desire to stop things from falling apart is frequently the driving force behind their decision. Clients say to me, "I want to stop drinking forever," but this is usually followed by something like, "but forever seems scary." Occasionally, I have met drinkers who have meant it when they said forever. Drinking has hurt them so badly that they can make this commitment, and the sheer black and white nature of the decision is something they are comfortable with. But having met thousands of drinkers, I know that those people who can make that unequivocal commitment to staying dry forever are few. For the vast majority who say *forever*, they know that's what they need but are very unsure they can achieve it.

If this describes you, I would like to suggest that you forget about giving up drinking forever. It's too much for your head to take in. That will send your subconscious into panic and it will start putting many negative thoughts in your head to sabotage you. My advice to you is to make a start with a length of time that you feel you can get your head around. Many of my clients have had success with an approach I call doubling-up. This is how it works:

To start, pick a period you think is realistic for you to achieve. It doesn't matter how long it is, providing you believe it's possible. But for the sake of this example, let's assume you choose the 10 days of this book's title as an initial target you think you can accomplish.

When you reach 10 days, decide what your next target will be. What can you achieve? Well, you have just done 10 days, so you know you have that one nailed – it's yours, you've just proved it. Therefore, why not do another 10 days? It can't be that hard if you have just done it, can it?

So you do another 10 days. That means you have 20 days in total under your belt. Well done! So what next? Well, as you now know you can do 20 days, you have that one ticked off, so how about another 20 days? You already know you can do it because you just have done it.

That brings you to 40 days, so you go for another 40 days and continue doubling up thereafter. The great thing about this strategy is that:

- Once you have done the first 10 days (or whatever initial target you choose) you will never again have to take on a target you haven't already done. That takes that strain out of staying sober. If you ever feel you are weakening, just say to yourself: "I've done this already."

- Pretty quickly, you will find that you are wonderfully comfortable about targeting periods of time that you would find alarming now.

- You can, if you keep doubling up, get to forever without ever having that as a target.

If you target forever, it can seem like a mountain to climb, and mountains are dangerous places that you can easily fall off. But using the simple doubling-up approach, you turn long-term sobriety into feeling more like a series of small hills you can easily walk up without breaking a sweat.

Your Alcohol Audit.

Note: As you are reading the print version of this book, please be aware that you will need online access to get the most from this chapter. If that is not convenient right now, come back to this chapter at another time.

In this book so far, I have made many references to heavy, moderate and light drinkers because a wide range of drinkers will find this book useful. Have you wondered which kind of drinker you are? Perhaps you think you know, or maybe you've had a debate going on in your head about which you are.

Well, it's time to find out.

We have an international system called Audit for assessing where people are at any one time on the spectrum of alcohol use. Audit (which stands for Alcohol Use Disorders Identification Test) is highly credible and used by the World Health Organization, so it gives us a science-backed standard to work with.

It doesn't matter whether you sip a glass of sherry once a year at Christmas or you down a pint of scotch for breakfast every day, there's a place for you on Audit. All you must do is answer a few questions and you get a score which tells you where you sit on the range of alcohol use. (This is different from the questionnaire in Chapter 2, which was for heavy drinkers wanting to assess their degree of dependency.)

You have ten multiple-choice questions to answer. (Yes, I know you can't see the questions yet, I'm coming to that.) For each question, you will score between 0 – 4, depending on your answer, so the maximum score possible for the whole ten questions is 40. Your score will tell you that you fall into one of the following categories:

- A score of 0 – 7. You are a light-to-moderate drinker. Although there is no safe level for alcohol consumption except zero, you are at low risk.
- A score of 8 – 15. You are an increasing-risk drinker. I would advise you to ease back on your drinking.
- A score of 16 – 19. You are a higher-risk drinker. You could develop alcohol dependence and alcohol-related problems. A score at this level should definitely be a wake-up call.
- A score of 20 – 40. You might already be a dependent drinker, and the higher in this range your score, the more at risk you are. You should refer to

the advice on reduction and seeking medical advice in Chapter 2 of this book.

The questionnaire is in the form of a table, and so that it is easy to read and print off copies, I have made it available for you as a PDF page that you can receive immediately to your email. So go and get a copy now but come back and read the rest of this chapter before you fill out your copy of Audit. The link you need to go to is subscribepage.com/free-pdf.

Okay, I hope you have now got a copy of Audit. If you can't find it in your email, check folders like "spam" or "promotions". If you still can't find it, try this alternative link: https://tinyurl.com/yxddcfck.

It's important when doing Audit that you answer every question. If none of the answers seems right for you, choose the one which sounds nearest to a correct reply. You can see how much to score each answer under where it says scoring system. You can choose only one answer for each of the 10 questions, so you should have a score of 0, 1, 2, 3, or 4 for each one.

Because this book will be read around the world, I have prepared a version of Audit that can work anywhere. In the questionnaire, you are asked about how much you drink (not surprisingly!) and this is complicated because different countries have different ideas of what a drink is. For example, many countries refer to a standard drink, which sounds simple enough, until you see that the level of alcohol in a standard drink varies from country to country. Also, some countries use imperial measures while others use metric. To cut through this potential confusion so that anyone reading this book can use Audit wherever they live, I have used a system called units of alcohol, which is an international standard, to define a single drink.

Across the top of the questionnaire, you will see examples of units of alcohol. For example, you will see that one measure of a spirit (which is about the amount that you would need to fill the bottle's cap) is about one unit, a bottle of wine is about 9 units, a pint of regular beer is 2 units, and so on.

The examples illustrated in the questionnaire should enable you to approximate how much you drink in units. If you are having any difficulty working out your units, try using the online calculator at https://tinyurl.com/yy4hlaze.

If you are intending to drink again after your detox break, alcohol units are useful to know about because they tell you how long you need to wait to be sober again, which is massively helpful if you are going for a drink today but need to drive tomorrow. A unit is the amount of alcohol the average person's body can process in an hour. So if you have drunk half a bottle of wine, which is about 4½ units, you know the alcohol will be out of your system in approximately 4½ hours' time.

Using Audit gives you clarity in understanding where you sit on the scale of alcohol use today. However, the score you get today is not the one you will have forever. Your Audit score will adjust over time to reflect changes in your alcohol consumption. Therefore, I recommend that you do Audit again every year to see if your score has changed. In this way, you have a way of keeping a check on your drinking, so you can use lowering your Audit score as a target to aim for in the future.

Day Six.

Nutrition and Weight Management.

Earlier in this book, I invited you to take a mind shift in relation to being sober. Rather than regarding sobriety as a challenge, I suggested that you should really see it as a place of comfort where you can feel nurtured and pampered. Sobriety is a safe place where you can get your life in balance, increase your happiness, feelings of self-worth, and improve your health.

My research into writing this book showed that improving nutrition and diet were major motivators for many people to reduce or stop drinking. Many of my clients have found that sobriety offers a great opportunity to improve their diet and therefore their physical and mental health.

Focusing on nutrition as a positive area in your life is better for your motivation than thinking of dealing with a negative problem like excessive drinking. If you think of sobriety purely in terms of not drinking, then you focus on something that's not actually there anymore, you see that there is a lack of something, you might feel that you are missing out, and that is demotivating.

119

Conversely, however, if you focus on improving your diet, you can make a mind shift and, instead of thinking of a lack, you can discover a new source of abundance in your life. Doesn't that feel better? Why focus on a lack when you can enjoy an abundance instead?

This can be especially important in those first 10 days of your sobriety when your body is detoxing. We routinely put habit-forming substances in our bodies, usually without questioning it. Most people often consume at least some of these: sugar, salt, caffeine, nicotine, prescription medications, recreational drugs, and of course alcohol. These can all be highly addictive. So when you cease putting one of these substances into your body, you will feel that something is missing because something really is, and it is a natural reaction to look for a substitute.

As cravings for a missing substance often feel like hunger, you might find you look to food as a substitute. This is why smokers notoriously put on weight when they quit, as cravings for nicotine feel like hunger. I remember that when I quit smoking, for several weeks afterwards, I ate like I was expecting a worldwide famine, but I reasoned that it was better for my health to put on some weight for a while than to keep smoking.

The good news for drinkers is that weight gain is not so likely to happen if you eat to replace alcohol. Smokers put on weight if they eat more because they are replacing a substance, nicotine, that contains zero calories. Alcohol, by comparison, is dripping with calories, so you can eat more without putting on weight.

I've worked with many drinkers who want to stop drinking because of weight problems, but not always because of excessive weight. Plenty of drinkers are underweight, even malnourished. So if alcohol has lots of calories, why is this?

With some people, drinking replaces proper eating, they skip meals altogether, and the drinker ends up painfully underweight and lacking in proper nutrition. When this happens, I think there are usually more complex issues going on with the individual, and drinking may well be a symptom of an eating disorder. Statistics show that 50% of people with eating disorders also have a diagnosable problem either with alcohol or another drug, and programs exist for dealing with eating and drinking disorders in tandem.

However, many drinkers are overweight, and it makes sense to point the finger of blame at the calories in alcohol. But it's often poor dietary choices made around drinking that cause at least as much trouble. For instance, let's take a typical evening drinker. A common scenario is drinking before eating in the evening. Then after a couple of drinks, the hunger pangs begin and the drinker starts snacking. The snacks available in pubs and bars are usually highly calorific, such as popular bar nibbles like peanuts, potato-based snacks, cheesy snacks, meaty snacks and chocolate bars. The drinker could easily consume more calories in food than in drink, all for minimal nutritional value. If that's then followed by a treble-stack super-mega bacon and cheeseburger with extra fries and soda on the way home, the evening calorie intake can run into thousands before you even add in the alcohol calories.

This is avoidable if the drinker has something to eat before having a drink. If you eat first, the urge to binge on calorific food later wouldn't happen. However, this is where alcohol causes poor eating choices, because it's instinctive with many drinkers to leave food till after that first drink, as food slows down the absorption of alcohol, which would delay that initial feeling of sedation that the drinker wants.

People who quit drinking to lose weight are often disappointed when the weight doesn't just fall off them. This is because, while they are consuming fewer calories, they are still consuming too many to lose weight, as they continue to overeat in other areas. They need to look at the whole of their diet, not just alcohol.

So, what sort of foods would it be good for you to eat? Well, a logical place to start would be with foods that can speed up your body's recovery from any damage that alcohol has caused.

Alcohol causes poor absorption of vitamins B1 (also known as thiamine) and B12, which is why if you have ever seen physicians about your drinking, they might have prescribed B vitamins. This is important to know. In extreme cases, a lack of B1 from heavy drinking can even cause irreparable brain damage, known as Wernicke-Korsakoff syndrome. I have met people with this and it's not pretty, but thankfully, it's totally preventable. Vitamin B12 is vital for your wellbeing. Vegans who drink should take note of this, as B12 can be scarce in an otherwise healthy vegan diet, so if alcohol is depleting the vegan's already low intake of B12, health problems could follow. Alcohol also affects the absorption of zinc, a vital mineral good for all a whole range of things, from your immune system to your sex life.

Here are foods that are good sources of B1, B12 and zinc.

- Legumes, which includes all kinds of beans, peas and lentils.
- Nuts and seeds.
- Oats.
- Oranges.
- Eggs.
- Lean meat and poultry.
- Fish and seafood.
- Fortified plant-based milk (the vegan B12 solution).

We have discussed alcohol's sedating effect on the brain, which drinkers find initially soothing. But this comes at a cost. Even small amounts of alcohol impair memory. Anyone who has ever drunk much will know that feeling of trying to remember what happened the night before, and regular alcohol use will shrink your brain. However, giving it a nutritional boost will help it recover. Good foods for your brain include:

- Omega-3 rich oily fish.
- Oranges and other citrus fruit.
- Beans, peas and lentils.
- Nuts, especially walnuts.
- Green tea.
- Avocados.

- Tomatoes.
- Ginger.

Alcohol gives your liver a bashing and can even lead to irreparable damage (sclerosis). An underperforming liver causes a range of problems, from chronic tiredness to weight-gain. So giving your liver a time-out to repair itself has to make sense. You can help it with foods high in sulfur and antioxidants. These include:

- Cruciferous vegetables, including cauliflower, broccoli, cabbage, and Brussels sprouts.
- Garlic and onions.
- All kinds of berries.
- Oranges, apples, plums, pears.
- Leafy green vegetables, especially spinach, rocket and collard greens.

Most fruit and vegetables contain antioxidants. My favourite tip is to choose ones that are darker and more colourful. Antioxidants give colour to food, so the more colour the food has, the more likely it is to be packed with antioxidants. So a red potato is better than a white one, and dark red lettuce is better than light green. Berries, like strawberries and blueberries, are more colourful than most other fruit, so they tend to be higher in antioxidants.

There are plenty of foods on the lists to choose from, so, whatever your tastes, there is no excuse not to eat at least some of them. But to get the maximum benefit, it's best to consider not just which foods to eat, but how to eat them. If it's possible to eat something just as it comes, then do that. For example, you are better eating whole fruit than drinking fruit juice, and better eating nuts as nature intended them, rather than processed into something else. For instance, blueberries are great, but if you put them in cakes, you will eat sugar, fats and additives as well.

As a rule of thumb, the less processed a food is, the better it is nutritionally. I like eating foods that have had nothing bad added and nothing good taken away. So if you cook a jacket potato in the oven, you have added nothing bad and taken nothing good away. But if you turn that potato into French fries, you have added bad things like cooking oil, salt and extra calories, and you have thrown away the nutrients in the peel. If you drink orange juice rather than eat oranges, you are throwing away all the highly-beneficial dietary fibre in the flesh of the fruit.

The way your body digests food, breaking it down into squidzillions of component nutrients and then distributing them among the cells in your body, is nothing short of amazing, and so complex that science doesn't yet know how it all works. Take, for example, phytonutrients. You might not have even heard of them. I must admit I hadn't until I started researching nutrition a few years ago. But they are vital to your immune system and your survival. Phytonutrients are micronutrients like vitamins and minerals. So far, science has documented over 10,000 of these. But we don't know what they all do or how many more are yet to be discovered, and we don't know how they all interact with each other and other nutrients. We just know that we'd be dead without them.

Because we need so many nutrients, it's best to eat a wide range of nutrient-rich foods, rather than focus on just a few or take supplements. That way you can be confident you are getting what you need, so you can relax about it, and just let your body get on with performing the daily miracle of digestion.

Adopting better eating habits will speed up your body's recovery from any damage alcohol might have done, so you will feel better quicker. Also, if you are planning to drink again in the future, by prioritizing the foods you have read about in this chapter, you will protect your body from the harmful effects of alcohol when you drink.

You will enjoy benefits beyond dealing with alcohol. For me, a major plus for having a healthy diet is that it takes away worry about sickness. I adopted a healthy eating lifestyle several years ago, and I know because of this I have reduced my chances of getting a nasty disease as I get older. My healthy eating habits massively boost my immune system. Also, on a day to day basis, irritating minor illnesses like colds, coughs and sore throats mostly leave me alone nowadays, as my body's defences see them off. I think that's a good reward for being selective about what I eat and how it's cooked.

If nutrition interests you, how about turning it into a MAP (meaningfully absorbing project)? There's more in my book "Change Your Life Today". If you want to go in-depth, I recommend the writings of Dr Michael Greger and Dr Joel Fuhrman, and the excellent not-for-profit website nutritionfacts.org.

Habits and Rituals.

You might think cravings are the number one problem that people face when they stop drinking. But in fact, this is not the case. At the outset, newly sober people struggle with cravings. But as we have already discussed, these cravings don't last long. They happen as the alcohol levels in your body drop, then when the alcohol level has fallen to zero, they stop soon afterwards. Your body gets used to the new reality.

During the time you have been drinking, however, you will have built up many habits and rituals around alcohol. These are a huge trigger to drink and a source of thought bombs. They are more powerful than cravings in the long term as they take far longer to shake off.

Not all habits are a problem, however. We all need them to navigate our way through our day-to-day lives. It's our autopilot. Without them, routine tasks would be a time-consuming challenge. When you brush your teeth in the morning, how do you do it? Probably you've never considered it, as you have a habit autopilot running it for you. Do you start on the left side, the right, or in the middle?

Where do you finish? How much toothpaste do you usually put on the brush? How long do you brush for? Likely, you have the same method, more or less, every day, but you would find it hard to remember what it is, without standing at the mirror with your toothbrush.

A habit is a program being run by your subconscious mind. It tells your body what to do so you can take appropriate action to perform whatever the task is. This leaves you clear to think with your conscious mind while the subconscious program runs. You do this all the time. If you are eating a meal while in conversation with someone, your habitual eating program, run by your subconscious, will take over so you can consciously focus on what you are saying and hearing. You can still cut up food and eat it without particularly thinking about it. You aren't going to accidentally put a carrot in your ear by mistake because you aren't concentrating on your eating.

These habitual programs develop with time. You didn't always know how to use a knife and fork. When you were born, your self-feeding program was much more basic. Over time, however, your subconscious learned, updated your program, and your feeding habits became much more refined.

Similarly, when you learned to ride a bike, swim, or hit a tennis ball, your mind started a new program and then updated it based on feedback. So, if you fell off your bike on the first attempt, your mind would have learned from what went wrong and updated the program running in your head. Then, after a while, you could cycle without having to think of the mechanics of what you were doing. You could balance and use the brakes and the gears hardly without thinking about it at all.

Your mind continuously learns from your actions and when you repeat an action, a new habit will evolve. The more you repeat the action, the more importance your mind will give to that habit. It becomes more ingrained, the neural pathway gets deeper, and the autopilot works better. This is why sportspeople will continuously practise the same movements, day after day, year after year. Whether they are kicking a ball, throwing a javelin, or shooting an arrow, they want to perfect the autopilot, as success lies in not having to think about the action as you do it. Pure habit is the goal.

This is all amazing. Your mind is a wonderful thing. Except, there is just one problem. Your mind will try to perfect the autopilot program of any repeated action. It doesn't discriminate between good and bad.

Just imagine for a moment you are someone who only drinks occasionally. Then one day, on your way to catch the train home from work, you stop at a shop and, on impulse, buy a can of beer to drink when you get home. Not a problem, right? But then, the next day, you're going past the same shop and you go in again and get another beer. "Hello," thinks your subconscious, "the action is being repeated, so this is important." The next day, you think you won't get a beer, but later you have the vague feeling that you miss it. This is your subconscious saying, "Haven't you forgotten something?"

So the following day, you pass by the shop again and buy a beer. You feel good about this because your mind has just let you have a little burst of dopamine into your system as a reward for repeating the action. You like that, so the next day you buy two beers.

You can see where this is going. From being someone who rarely drinks, you could, in a matter of weeks, end up becoming a daily drinker buying a four-pack every night.

Two things are happening here. Not only are you getting that little feeling of sedation that you like when you take your first drink, but your mind is also giving you a hit of dopamine before you even have the drink as a reward for repeating the behaviour. Dopamine is one of the feel-good drugs that your body produces naturally. It feels nice. Your body releases dopamine to encourage you to perfect this new habit. It doesn't realize that it's potentially bad for you. Your mind is non-judgemental in this respect.

Have you ever had the feeling that you really need a drink? Yes, I'm sure you have, or you probably wouldn't be reading this. But how did you feel when you bought your drink and the barman was pouring it? Or when you picked up the bottle of wine from the supermarket shelf? Did you feel better already? Probably you did, as the dopamine reward would happen. You got a reward before you drank the drink.

How about when you had that first drink? Did you get that feeling of intoxication almost as soon as you took the first sip? Probably. That's what most people say. But hold on here. It takes alcohol anything up to half an hour to be absorbed into the body. It has to reach your stomach, fight its way through any food there, then get absorbed through the stomach's lining, pass into the bloodstream and reach your brain.

So how can you feel intoxicated before the alcohol has reached your brain? The answer seems to be that because

133

your mind knows what's coming, it can recreate that feeling before it really happens. If your mind believes you are drinking alcohol, it will run that program and create the effect of becoming progressively drunk, even if you are not drinking alcohol. Having the belief that you are drinking can affect your judgment and your memory. We know this is possible because of scientific tests using placebo alcoholic drinks.

Researchers at the University of Victoria in New Zealand found this when they ran a test on 148 students. They gave them all drinks, told half the students they were drinking vodka and tonic and told the other half they were drinking tonic water only. In reality, they were all drinking flat tonic water with lime. To recreate a drinking ambience, the experiment took place in a room that looked like a bar, and they gave them the flat tonic water from vodka bottles.

Later, the researchers showed pictures of a crime scene to the students and asked questions about it. They found that the students who believed they had drunk vodka had a poorer recollection of events and were less reliable as witnesses. The belief that they were intoxicated resulted in real symptoms of intoxication – not surprising if their mind was running the program of how they habitually reacted when they were intoxicated.

If you observe how people behave when they're drinking, you see that they usually go through the same steps in the same order. Someone might start off seeming very cheerful, then become sentimental – perhaps to the point of being weepy for no reason – then become feisty and belligerent, again for no reason. That person will probably run through the same sequence every time they drink heavily, as that is how their habitual program plays out. Someone else might start out being loud and telling jokes, then become sullen and withdrawn, and finish the evening by storming out believing, for no good reason, that the world is against them. That's just the way their habitual program plays out.

You can probably recognize this in yourself. You repeat the same behaviours when you've been drinking, although alcohol's effects on the memory make it difficult to remember what you do in the later stages of intoxication. Most drinkers will know the experience of the end of the evening being a total blank. Some of my clients have experienced having whole days that were blank.

But it's not just when you drink that your habitual programs run. They are running in your life all the time. One that you will be familiar with is how you react when you want a drink. This is deeply habitual. With drinkers who abstain during the week but binge at the weekend, the urge to drink will

135

start building from midweek, reaching a crescendo at the end of work on Friday. With daily drinkers, it usually starts at the same time every day. The thought will come into your head, and it becomes a craving.

As you are now a few days into your detox, you will no doubt have experienced this to some extent. You will have been expecting this, I hope, so it won't have been a surprise. As we have also already discussed, the physical cravings, triggered as the level of alcohol in the system drops, will dissipate during the detox period.

But at this point, I must warn you that the cravings won't just stop when you have finished your detox. Your mind can run your "I need a drink" program anytime. Although these cravings are in the mind, you will feel them physically. Usually, the craving will accompany an obvious trigger. Say you see an ad for your favourite drink, you won't be surprised to get a craving, so you can take evasive action, like focusing on your Meaningfully Absorbing Project (MAP) or urge surfing.

This kind of craving causes trouble particularly when it seems entirely random. You are happily breezing through your day when out of nowhere a massive urge to drink hits you. There is no warning or build-up. Suddenly – wham –

there it is. This can put the sober person into a tailspin as they were unprepared and don't know what to do. They often feel panic. But don't panic. This happens. When I have been counselling someone this has happened to, I usually find that when the client thinks back carefully, they spot a trigger. But at the time it was subtle, and they didn't take any notice, so were caught off-guard.

The trigger could be something as small as a snippet of an overheard conversation about drinking, passing someone in the street you've seen in a bar, or maybe a song on the radio that you have heard in your local watering-hole. It could even have been something you dreamed of – it's common for ex-drinkers to have drinking dreams.

That little trigger did nothing at the time, and on a conscious level you had forgotten about it. But your subconscious hadn't forgotten, and hours or maybe even days later, it unexpectedly starts running the program of how you habitually feel when you want a drink.

So when this happens – and it will – don't worry. It's just your subconscious selecting the wrong program to run. The longer you stay sober, the less often it will happen.

Rituals

A ritual is again an ingrained habit, but with an extra layer of meaning. Rituals define who we are.

Let's take eating, for example, which is a ritual we take part in every day. When you eat, do you sit on a chair or the floor? Do you eat with cutlery, chopsticks, or your fingers? The culture you identify with will determine how you eat, and every time you eat that way, you are reinforcing your identification with that culture. The food you choose will also determine who you are. In my country, the tradition is to eat turkey at Christmas. But if I go to Portugal, the locals cook cod and octopus dishes at that time of year. It defines their identity.

Sport is very ritualistic. Just look at the supporters at a big sporting event. It's their ritual to dress in their team's colours, maybe even painting their faces, and singing or chanting to define their identity with a particular side. International events will define your nationality.

Work for most people is a major ritual in their lives. It follows strict rules of conduct, dress, and even when you can have personal freedom. Many people don't just go to work, they fuse with their role to such an extent that it becomes their identity. This is especially true of people who stay in

138

the same job for years. I have worked with many clients who have lost their job or retired and, as a result, have had a personality crisis – they have lost their sense of self because it was so wrapped up with their working persona. They have a deep sense of loss and often turn to alcohol because they don't know what else to do, which is why they end up in my consulting room.

There are many variations of the drinker's persona: the sophisticated wine buff, the one-of-the-boys drinker, the girl-on-the-town drinker, the street drinker, the sporting event drinker, the after-work drinker, and many more. Drinkers who have fused with their drinking identity will feel that their sense of self is on the line if they give up alcohol.

In particular, drinkers who feel they are being forced into quitting will tenaciously hang on to their drinking identity and rituals as a justification to keep drinking. They will resist like crazy if a partner, doctor, or authority figure tries to change them. If they are forced to change, they will experience that same profound sense of loss that someone who loses a long-term job will experience. They will develop a major resentment towards whoever made them stop. And people with a resentment aren't committed to staying sober.

On the contrary, they are looking for any excuse to backslide.

So what is your drinking identity? What rituals do you go through when you drink? Drinking has many rituals. You will have your own. It could be the type of alcohol you buy, how you store it, when you drink it, or who you drink it with.

- Do you drink with the boys at the rugby club or the women at the country club?
- Do you drink fine wine from a fancy glass in a snazzy restaurant, or Budweiser out of the can while you're flat out on the couch watching television?
- Do you always drink three beers and then switch to scotch?
- Do you insist on drinking wine only from one particular grape variety?
- Do you always meet the same friends for a drink on Friday night and experience a sense of loss if you can't get there?
- Do you always sit on the same barstool and get annoyed if someone has taken it already?
- Have you fused with your drinking identity or can you let it go?

If you have difficulty leaving your drinking identity behind during your detox, try considering what you would like your identity to look like. So instead of mourning the loss of your drinking self, take a mind shift and see the opportunity to become who you want to be. How would you like the world to see you? Do you want the world to see you as someone who drinks a lot? Probably not, as you have had the insight to read this book. More likely you want the world to see you as a more positive, fitter and happier person.

So what exactly do you want the new you to look like? What benefits do you want sobriety to bring? What other improvements are you looking for? If you don't have a clear idea already, I suggest grabbing your notepad and writing down what comes into your head. Then you can refine it until you see the true you that you really want. What does that look like? Take a mind shift now and focus on that future you rather than your old drinker image. You don't need that old version of yourself anymore. It has served you for some time but doesn't serve you anymore. You can safely discard that old you now. It's time to move on.

If you struggle to nail down exactly what you want in life, this can be a problem. Many people only think of what they don't want, such as they don't want to drink so much. But without a clear picture of what you do want, you might struggle with motivation. If you are such a person and have difficulty knowing what you want, take a look at the appendix at the end of this book. It's an extract from my book "Change Your Life Today" that deals with the issue of finding a positive life purpose. I hope you find it useful.

When you have an idea in mind of what you want that new post-alcohol you to look like, consider what that person will do. What will be the new rituals in your life that will replace the old ones? I think it's interesting that alcohol treatment services for chronic drinkers are very structured, offering the client ways of replacing their former selves. 12-Step treatment is particularly noteworthy for having a highly structured and ritualistic methodology. Essentially, it offers the drinker an all-encompassing, off-the-shelf new identity. This can work remarkably well for some people. But I think its weakness is that it's like a clothing store that only stocks one size, and if that size doesn't fit you, you will not buy.

You, however, are free to choose what fits you, so have fun with this new sober self. You can decide which habits and rituals work for you and help you become the person you want to be.

Day Seven.

The Flow Practice.

In this chapter, I want to introduce you to a technique that is a pleasure to use and will help you de-stress, handle thoughts about drinking, and add to your feeling that being sober is a safe and nurturing place where life becomes easier.

Sound good? Let's dive in.

Earlier in the book, we looked at a relaxation technique that I hope you found helpful. I want now to take this a step further and show you how your cares and stresses can literally float away.

A few years ago, I came across a relaxation meditation called *Leaves on a Stream*. It worked well for me and, more importantly, got a big thumbs-up from my clients, too. I have since developed this into a relaxation that you can call upon anytime life gets stressy, or even just when you want to use it for enjoyment, as it's rather lush for your head. I used it myself last night when I woke up in the night to help me get back to sleep. It has many uses. As I have changed the original quite a lot, I have renamed it *The Flow Practice*.

Before we have a go, I need you to do a bit of visualization. I want you to imagine a stream or small river. This river can be one of your invention, or it can be one that really exists, it doesn't matter. But what is important is that it's somewhere you feel comfortable. So it will probably be a river in a part of the world that you like. It might be in a peaceful country setting, but it could be a stream in a town if that appeals to you. Imagine you are sitting by a tree next to the river. Try to build up a detailed image in your mind. If your river is a real one near where you live, it might help to go there soon and note the details.

When I do this exercise, I imagine a small, shallow river in a verdant field in the English countryside. The day is warm. It's quiet apart from the sounds of birds, the occasional noise of cattle in the distance, and the sound of the water. It's somewhere I feel comfortable and at peace with the world. Your river might be quite different – whatever works for you is fine. Some people are better than others at visualizing, so if you aren't getting a lot of detail, just focus on your river flowing.

Once you have decided what your river looks like, get yourself comfortable on a chair, couch or bed, at a time when you will be undisturbed. I suggest you set a timer, so you don't have to look at your watch. You could try starting with five minutes, or maybe ten minutes if you are experienced at relaxation or meditation exercises, then increase the length of the practice a little every time you do this exercise. It's usually helpful to close your eyes.

Next, turn your attention to your breathing. Put your hand on your stomach and feel if it rises and falls when you breathe. If it doesn't, that means you are just breathing into your chest rather than your diaphragm, which is anxious, shallow breathing. If that's how it is, try imagining that you are breathing into your belly, and you should start breathing deeper. But don't force it. As you relax, your breathing will become slower and deeper of its own accord.

Next, let your body feel loose and heavy. Imagine you are melting into the surface below you. You might find it helps to imagine this as a progressive movement along your body, so start with your feet. Imagine your heels melting into the surface below them and then move up your body to the top of your head, imagining the same thing. Pay particular attention to your shoulders. Let them sag as much as you can, then let them sag even more. The sensation of feeling loose and relaxed should be a pleasant one, so smile if you like. If you still feel tense, that's a sign that you need to do this regularly.

147

Relaxation is something we can all do from birth, but during your life, as you learn to be tense, you might lose the knack of relaxing and have to learn how to do it. Drinkers in particular find it hard to relax if they have got used to opening a bottle and using sedation instead of real relaxation to unwind.

The first time you do this exercise, you might find you want to rush on to the next step. But after a while, you will probably find that you want to slow down and just enjoy the sensation of feeling loose and relaxed. Then, when you are ready, bring to mind your river.

Imagine the scene in detail. What vegetation is along the riverbank? What is the weather like? Can you feel the sun on your skin or the breeze? Are you alone or are there any people around? Are there animals or birds? What can you smell? What can you hear? How are you dressed? How fast is the river flowing? How deep is that water and is it clear? Can you see fish? Is it flowing around rocks or over gravel? Is there a weir? Try to get a full picture. Take as long as you like.

Notice that leaves are floating along with the flow.

When you next have a thought or a feeling, imagine you are putting that thought or feeling on a leaf and watching it float

148

away until it's out of sight. So, if you've had a hard day at work and the thought "I hate my boss" comes to mind, put that thought on a leaf and watch it float away. You could imagine the words "I hate my boss" standing on the leaf if you like, or you might imagine your boss reduced to a tiny size and standing on the leaf – whatever works for you. If you suddenly think, "I need a drink", imagine those words appearing on a leaf and then floating away. If you feel a strong emotion, let's say anger, imagine the word anger on a leaf and watch it float away. Chances are that the emotion will come back, but just keep putting it on a leaf as often as necessary. If a thought bomb pops up in your mind, put that on a leaf. You might imagine it as a cartoon bomb with a smouldering fuse.

Continue doing this with any thought or feeling that comes to mind. It doesn't matter whether it's a good or bad thought, put it on the next leaf. If the habits or rituals we discussed previously come to mind, put them on a leaf. You might even think something like, "This is a waste of time", but just put it on a leaf. And if your mind wanders off, let's say you get wrapped up in thinking about what's for dinner, when you realize that you've drifted off, go back to your river and put "Dinner" on a leaf.

149

When your timer goes off, let your river gradually fade away, slowly open your eyes, and take in whatever is in front of you. Have a stretch, maybe wiggle your toes and fingers, and reconnect with your day.

The benefit you get from this practice is very much dose-responsive, so the more often you do it, the better you will feel, and the better you will be able to deal with any temptation to break your sobriety. It will become more apparent as you continue through this book just how useful it is. If you do this practice once a month, you're not going to get much from it. If you do it every day, it's likely to become a core part of your life to help you deal with many life issues, not just drinking.

In doing this practice, you are developing the skill of being able to observe your thoughts and feelings as if they are separate from you. Most people don't. Most people just experience their thoughts and feelings and then react based on their old habits. This is why most drinkers reach for a drink when something goes wrong – the subconscious runs 'drinking' as the go-to program in this instance. But if you can see the thought or feeling, rather than just react, you can take control and run the program of your choice.

I ran a training group for this practice. Here is the feedback from one participant, which makes the benefits clearer:

"When I first tried the practice, I was in a room with other people, which seemed a bit weird, and I didn't think it would work, as I was too aware of everyone else. Also, I had tried relaxation and meditation before without success. I just couldn't settle and would get bored and want to go and do something. But to my surprise, in this training, I really drifted off into my own world. When we finished the practice and I opened my eyes, I had the sense of surfacing from a very deep place inside of me.

We were targeted to repeat the practice 6 times over the following week at home for 10 minutes each time. I got really into it and looked forward to it. I'm not the best at visualizing, so I had a really simple little river, with a bend in it. It always flowed from left to right. When I got a thought, I imagined it as a written word on a leaf. So if the thought of paying a bill came to mind, I would put the word 'money' on a leaf and watch it float downstream. When it disappeared around the corner, I would just wait for the next thought.

I had heard of this idea of looking at your thoughts before but didn't understand it. I couldn't see how it was possible.

Using the leaf idea made it simple. The thing that struck me most was that my thoughts were very random. They didn't come in any logical sequence at all, which just shows how chaotic your thinking can be.

After a while, I found that I could conjure up my river in my head any time I liked. If I was in a hurry but needed some help, I didn't need to go through the relaxation routine first. So if I was out and about and suddenly got hit by the urge to drink, I could imagine my river, then put the word 'urge' on a leaf and watch it float off. This showed me that it was just a thought, and I gradually started to understand that when I had a thought, I didn't need to act on it. If I wanted to, I could just put the thought on a leaf and let it float off.

This was revolutionary stuff for me. In the past, I had always been the kind of person to react off-the-cuff without any kind of plan to any difficult thoughts that came to mind, which was bad news for me because that reaction usually involved a drink. But the practice helps me stay off the drink and helps me with other situations as well. It keeps me calm and helps me react to situations calmly rather than just firing from the hip all the time."

Movement.

Because alcohol is a sedative, it makes you feel less energetic, and this effect carries on after the period of intoxication has passed. If you are an occasional drinker, you must have noticed that after a night on the booze, the following morning you feel lethargic. And if you have had a binge, perhaps over the weekend, it can take as much as three days for you to feel back to full fettle, especially as you get older.

If you drink daily or nearly every day, you might be so used to that lethargic feeling that you think it's how you are naturally, because you don't stay away from alcohol long enough for the effects to wear off. You might have thought your lack of energy was because of ageing, when in fact it's just the effect of alcohol. I have known drinkers to take supplements, change their diets or join a gym to feel fitter when all they need to do is take a few days off the booze.

By now, you should be far enough into your detox to get more energetic. To what degree you are feeling livelier will depend on several factors like how much you have been drinking, over what period of time, and your general level of

153

fitness in relation to your age. But even if you've been hammering the drink, you should at least be feeling somewhat sprightlier, so it's time to look at getting more movement into your life. This is important to your sobriety and general happiness. Here's why:

- Drinking is largely sedentary. If you spend many hours a week teetering on a barstool with your Chardonnay or lying on the couch with a beer balancing on your belly, then you will be used to being inactive. Breaking your old routines is as vital as not drinking, and often doing the opposite of what you usually do is the way to go. So getting active when you were habitually inactive makes sense.

- Alcohol will have affected your brain chemistry and you might have become more prone to low moods. However, building more movement into your day now will encourage your brain to release your body's natural feel-good chemicals in your head, like endorphins and serotonin, so you will feel happier. That's got to be good.

- As you become more energetic, you will naturally want to move about more, and being more active will help your body recalibrate quicker. So if, for

154

example, you find you are having difficulty sleeping since you started detoxing, then getting more exercise will help to settle you into a new sleep pattern, and the quality of your sleep will be better and more refreshing than alcohol-induced sleep.

So what kind of exercise should you be doing? Well, when people stop drinking, they often take up running, swimming, or working out at the gym, and these are all great things to do. But often people do an intensive burst of these kinds of exercises a few times a week and feel they have done all they need and go back to being sedentary at other times, which goes a long way to cancelling out their efforts. What makes the biggest impact is being active routinely and often during your day, so you are moving to some extent the majority of the time.

This can be difficult if you have an office job. At the last outpatient unit I worked at, I spent a lot of time in a chair, either while talking to clients or typing up notes and doing emails. But I tried to compensate by parking a mile from the hospital, so at least I had a walk twice a day. If I was running a therapy group, I would stand up throughout, rather than spend 90 minutes in a chair. When I had phone calls, I would walk around while I talked. At the moment, writing this book presents a challenge as it's undeniably sedentary.

155

But if I am thinking about how to phrase something or what my next topic will be, I'll walk around as I think rather than just stare at the screen.

Walking is probably the best form of exercise you can get if you do enough of it and at a reasonable pace. 3 miles an hour would be a good benchmark. I need to walk at least four miles daily, or I don't sleep well. Four miles isn't a lot if you're used to doing it.

One aspect of walking that should interest drinkers is its beneficial effects on the brain. You know that alcohol affects your brain, impairing your balance and judgment, eroding your memory and altering your mood. So if you consider how many hours a week you spend intoxicated, you will get an idea of how much time your brain spends being blitzed by alcohol. But walking and other forms of aerobic exercise send essential nourishing molecules to the brain, which over time will help heal the damage that alcohol has done.

Here's the experience of one client:

"I was a heavy drinker for years and when I gave up, my mind was all over the place and I couldn't sleep. So I started walking. I left my truck parked in the yard and just walked. I live in a rural area, so I would walk to the next village, then eventually I was walking to the county town

156

and back, a 20-mile round trip. I didn't care about the weather. I bought a fantastic high-tech rain jacket which kept off the rain without making me hot, and with over-trousers and good boots, I was my own mobile microclimate, so the weather didn't bother me.

Over the first few months of sobriety, I walked hundreds of miles. It worked. My physical health was fantastic, and I slept like a baby. But what I really appreciated was the upturn in my mental health. Anxiety and depression had troubled me for years. It all vanished within months. I realized that it had all been alcohol-related, which is ironic as I drank because I was depressed. It was only later that I understood that I was depressed because I drank!"

Day Eight.

Emotional Thinking.

So far, we have looked at three key triggers for drinking that could undermine your sobriety.

Firstly, we discussed physical cravings for alcohol and how your brain can continue to manufacture these feelings long after the alcohol has left your body. Secondly, we looked at thought bombs and how they can hit you out of the blue. Thirdly, we looked at how habitual behaviours and rituals create a strong link to your drinking past. We now come to the last of the major triggers. I have saved it until last because it's a biggie: emotional thinking.

I cannot begin to estimate how many times I have seen someone get drunk because of an emotional meltdown. One day they would look good, well-presented, all smiles, and positive about their sobriety. Then the next time you see them, they fall through the door in disarray after drinking again. What sets off this dramatic downturn in events? The most common reasons are rows with partners and family, run-ins with authority figures, and anything that causes a sense of outrage and injustice.

Earlier in this book, we discussed how the default setting of most drinkers is to reach for a drink in emotionally upsetting situations. This idea is rooted deep in popular thinking. Many people still believe that a drink of brandy, for example, is good for emotional shock, so if someone has a disturbing situation and says, "I need a drink", it's unlikely to be questioned.

Indeed, that initial feeling of sedation when you have a drink might help for a few minutes, but pretty soon that slight feeling of calmness turns into a greasy slope down which you can slide mighty quickly if you keep drinking. Alcohol exaggerates negative feelings. So a couple of hours later, far from feeling happier, you could be sobbing uncontrollably into your gin and tonic or going into a rage at the injustice you feel has been done to you.

I suggested earlier that rather than reaching for a drink in an emotionally upsetting situation, it makes far more sense to reach for your sobriety. If you are sober, you will be in a far fitter state to deal with whatever is going on in your life. Once you take action, you will most likely feel calmer and less emotional. If you need more help, you can use the relaxation techniques you have learned in this book.

However, although reaching for your sobriety makes far more sense than reaching for a drink, you might not do it. Why? Because the power of that entrenched habit to have a drink is massively compelling, it's probably been your emotional reflex since adolescence. It's a deeply cut neural pathway, and it will not vanish instantly.

Consequently, when you find yourself in an emotional situation, the reflex to drink will kick in as your default so fast that you could forget the concept of reaching for sobriety instead. You might remember later, but if you've just knocked back your third tequila slammer at that point, it's a bit late.

Alternatively, you might remember about staying sober before you pick up a drink, but the sheer force of habit overrides good sense and makes you have a drink anyway, even though you know that it's the wrong thing to do. This is a phenomenon that my counselling clients find so frustrating: the habit bullies them into doing something that they intellectually know is self-defeating.

Many feelings can trip you up, but there are a few that crop up time and again. I think at the head of the queue are resentments. It has been said many times in treatment services that having a resentment is like drinking poison hoping to hurt the other guy. Resentments are toxic and self-defeating. When someone does something you see as an injustice, resentment will follow. It's a painful feeling that gnaws away at you and keeps you awake. You might even have fantasies about revenge. That's when the thought bombs start hitting you with messages like, "They shouldn't treat you like that. It's outrageous. You deserve a drink. Who wouldn't have a drink in that situation?" And so on. It's challenging to let go of these powerful emotions. Yet many resentments aren't necessary and are often entirely preventable because they result from wishful thinking.

I had a couple visit me who had been drinking heavily since they retired: Aylene and Max. Aylene explained that in the past they had drunk a lot when they were on holiday but had always reined it in when they got back to work. However, they had sold a business and had retired together in their mid-fifties and had been drinking like life was a holiday ever since. It was her wish that she and her husband cut down and stop before it affected their health. Aylene was ready for change. She'd had enough.

Max, however, was clearly there against his will. He even said that Aylene had "dragged" him to my office and that he had only agreed to see me "to keep her happy". But clearly, he wasn't keeping her happy. They argued. She

164

cried. Max stonewalled me, determined that no fancy-pants therapist would come between him and his brandy. After a few minutes, he left in a strop, saying he needed a drink. But Aylene stayed and after she had composed herself, we started to work on a plan for her.

We discussed that Max simply wasn't ready for change and that if she tried to pressurise him, he would just become even more defensive and wedded to his drink. But although that was unhelpful, it didn't stop Aylene from helping herself. She cut down and then stopped drinking altogether, which seemed to suit her. She said she felt years younger, and she hoped that Max might follow her example. Then after a month, she started drinking again. It turned out that under the calm exterior she showed when I saw her, she had a seething resentment against Max for not stopping with her. You can understand the emotional pain she had, but by drinking again, she was being self-defeating – she had drunk the poison wanting to hurt the other guy.

It would be easy to lay the blame on Max, but at least he had been clear in his desire to keep drinking. Where the resentment had come from was in Aylene's wishful thinking that he would suddenly change. It was an unrealistic expectation that would bring her pain when she saw it would not happen.

We talked about this and that while at best she could only influence Max, she was in total charge of herself. If she could let go of her wishful thinking, she could let go of the resentment. This might seem unfair on Aylene. But if she took responsibility for her health and happiness, rather than giving all the power to Max, she could move on from drinking and the fear of ill health, and find some peace of mind. Aylene began to see that, while blaming Max was the instinctive thing to do, if she took responsibility for herself, she would take back the power to control her wellbeing.

Aylene stopped drinking again. The last time I saw her, Max had started taking nalmefene, a medication to help him cut down, so her good example had worked in the end.

A bitter sense of injustice that life is unfair and you are a victim leads also to resentment's toxic sibling: self-pity. A few years ago, I was working on outreach, which means I was being sent out into the community. That's where I met Colin, a new client. Colin rented a house in a pleasant market town in southern England, the sort of pretty, peaceful place many people aspire to live in. Colin's head, however, was in a place that was neither pretty nor peaceful.

Colin was in his forties. He always dressed in the same pair of ripped jeans – not ripped in a fashionable way, just ripped – and a faded sweatshirt. His house was austere in the extreme. He passed most of his time sitting in an old armchair in the middle of an otherwise sparsely furnished living room. This was where Colin spent his days, lamenting how life had treated him so unfairly.

Sure enough, bad things had happened in his life, but nothing that doesn't happen to most of us. He had a failed marriage behind him, but it seemed that his wife, who still looked in to see if he was all right, had become exhausted by his self-pity. He had lost his job and lived on benefits. Although he was capable of work, he wasn't being offered work that he felt was good enough for him, which was a clue to Colin's true calamity in life: he wasn't living the life he thought should be his. He was angry at the world for treating him so badly. His life didn't meet his expectations. When we discussed where Colin's expectations came from, however, he couldn't say. They were just there in his head, firing out thought bombs.

The upshot was that when Colin had money, he bought whiskey, which he drank alone, sitting on his old armchair. Isolating with alcohol in his ditch of self-pity, Colin was trapped in a world that he believed didn't care. Then, when

167

he was thoroughly miserable and drunk, he would go out walking. He would trip over and hurt himself enough to need patching up in a hospital, which is how he came to the attention of our services.

Although Aylene's and Colin's stories are very different, they have a common denominator: they were both the victims of their own expectations. Aylene expected her husband to stop drinking with her, although she had no reason to believe that he might. In fact, Max had been quite clear that he wanted to continue drinking. Colin had expectations that his life should be better, but with no basis for that belief. Their episodes of excess drinking were merely a symptom of their unrealistic expectations, so the bitter resentments they felt were of their own invention. They had been thinking with their emotions, not their logical brains.

I believe that when most people find they are drinking too much or find they can't stop drinking, it results from some unrealistic, emotional thinking. Taking a drink to deal with misguided ideas makes no more sense than changing a lightbulb because you're hungry. But where alcohol is involved, our common-sense deserts us – it's extraordinary.

So what's the answer? If drinking is a symptom of poor thinking, should we all get cognitive therapy? Well, it would help! But this is a book about taking a 10-day detox, not root-and-branch therapy. Is there a quick solution to all this dodgy thinking?

In fact, we already touched on part of the solution in the Flow Practice. You will recall that you took any thoughts or feelings that came to mind and put them on a leaf. You could imagine the thought or feeling like a word on the leaf. So if you felt angry, you could put the word "angry" on a leaf and let it float off.

Being able to look at your feelings and identify them like that is a fabulous skill that can help you handle emotionally charged situations which usually see you reaching for a drink. The act of looking at your feelings objectively and being able to label them creates a pause that might just give you time to prioritize sobriety. This is important, and here's a little neuroscience to explain why:

Emotional responses come from the amygdala and other limbic areas of your brain. This is the oldest part of your brain in evolutionary terms and is at the back of your head. If these areas of your brain are in charge, you can get buffeted about by your emotional reactions to whatever is happening in your life, making you more likely to pick up a drink.

The location of the logical part of your brain is in the frontal cortex – that's at the front of your head, and where you do your conscious thinking. Having a frontal cortex is a key difference between us and other primates. Humans have developed a near vertical forehead to make space for the frontal cortex. But other primates have sloping foreheads because they don't have the same highly developed logical part of the brain to accommodate in the skull. In simple terms, if you are thinking with the front of your head, logic is in charge. But if you're thinking with the back of your head, your emotions are in charge, so you're thinking with your feelings rather than your common sense.

When drinkers are trying to get sober, these two parts of the brain are often in conflict, and if the emotional area of the brain is winning the battle, this explains why drinkers can find that they drink (an emotional response coming from the limbic area) even though they know better (because the frontal cortex tells them it's a bad idea). This is an uncomfortable state of mind to be in. The fancy name for this is *cognitive dissonance*: you know something is bad for you, but you do it anyway. It can feel like you are going a little crazy because you know it makes no sense. But somehow you can't stop your actions from undermining you.

If the frontal cortex has the upper hand, however, you can control your emotions better and do what makes sense. The act of naming your emotions, known as affect labelling, helps put the logical part of your brain in charge. Using an amazing brain-scanning technology that has emerged in recent years called functional magnetic resonance imaging, scientists found that naming your emotions slows down the emotional responses from the limbic areas of your brain. This gives the frontal cortex more of a chance to take charge, helps you cope better with negative feelings, and makes you less likely to break your sobriety when something upsets you.

Being able to name your feelings is a knack. At first, it can seem testing. But when you get the knack, it's simple. If you struggle with it, try the Flow Practice again and imagine putting the name of your emotion on a leaf. If you can do that, you've cracked it.

You can try out your new skill today. Notice what feelings crop up as you go through your day and label them. It doesn't matter what they are, good or bad, just notice what comes up and give it a name: happy, confused, timid, brave,

171

bored, stubborn, relieved, fearful, sad, joyous, excited, embarrassed, overwhelmed, passionate, jealous, lonely, absorbed, frustrated, tranquil – whatever. There is no right or wrong, as you will go through a wide range of emotions in an ordinary day.

If you would like to look in greater depth at how to control your emotions, I recommend my book *"The Emotional Mind: Overcome Anxiety, Stress, Negativity and Procrastination"*, which develops many of the concepts you have met in this book.

James and Susanna.

As you are getting close to the end of your 10 days, you might think about where you are going with your escape into sobriety. It's always useful to hear from people who have already experienced what you are doing, so let's look at two people who are a few weeks further down the road from where you are at present: James and Susanna. They are both following the type of strategies you have read about in this book, but they are looking for different outcomes. James wants a fixed-term break from alcohol, while Susanna is thinking long-term.

We'll hear from James first:

"I am, by nature, the kind of person who likes routine, and this is how I drink. A normal day for me would be to have a beer or a small glass of wine during my lunch break from work. Then on my way home, I stop by my local. This is a sociable thing for me. I live in the area where I was brought up and know most people, so there are always people for me to chat to, often people I went to school with twenty years ago. While I'm in my local, I habitually have two pints of beer. Then I walk home, where I share a bottle of

wine in the evening with my wife. At the weekend, my routine is similar, but I usually slip in a few extra drinks, and on Sunday lunchtime, I usually have a few.

I've never regarded this as abnormal. I have never been a problem drinker – at least I don't think so. I might get a bit wobbly at times, but I never get really drunk. I never drink whiskey or any spirits. I don't drink alone or do any of the sorts of things you associate with problem drinkers.

Then I had a health check. My blood pressure was high. The nurse asked me about my drinking. I answered her honestly. She said I was drinking nearly 100 units of alcohol a week. I didn't know what a unit was. She said that a unit was equivalent to a single shot of whiskey. That hit home for me. I would regard anyone who was drinking 100 whiskeys a week as having a serious problem, yet I was drinking the same amount of alcohol myself, just in a different form. I needed to do something. The nurse referred me to a counsellor, who helped me get a strategy.

I couldn't get my head around just quitting, so I started to cut down, bit by bit. I couldn't be doing with counting units, that seemed just too clinical. So I started to chip away at my routine drinks. I started by cutting out the lunchtime drink. To be honest, I knew in the back of my mind that drinking at lunchtime wasn't good, and I didn't have too much difficulty cutting that out.

Then I cut out one of my pints on the way home. That was more difficult. But I got used to it after a few days and then cut out both pints. That was tough because it meant I couldn't visit my local, which meant I didn't get the social contact I was used to. But I just couldn't visualize me standing at the bar with a fruit juice in my hand. So, as it was summer, I started going for a walk after work instead. That turned out to be sociable anyway, as I bumped into old mates I hadn't seen for ages. My wife sometimes came with me, so it was good for our relationship. And as a bonus, I realized just what a lovely area I live in and started to wonder why I had wanted to spend so much time in a pub, anyway.

That just left me with the wine in the evening. I decided the time had come to go for it and stop drinking completely. I hoped the combination of walking and not drinking would bring my blood pressure down.

The first 10 days were difficult. But I focused on walking, counting my steps on a pedometer rather than lamenting my lack of alcohol. I found the relaxation exercises were good to help me sleep, and after a few days I was sleeping *like a log. The concept of thought bombs was amazing. Whenever the voice in my head tries to drag me off the rails, I just think, "Oh, it's just one of those thought bombs", and I can move on. At the end of the 10 days, I decided to commit to 3 months – enough time, I hope, to turn my health around. After then, I plan to drink again, but much less than before. I'll decide when I reach 3 months. Who knows? I might decide to do another 3 months."*

Now let's hear Susanna's experience:

"I am, without a doubt, an emotional drinker. I can be absolutely fine when I have my first drink, but by the third, I start to become all sentimental. It's mad. I get sentimental about things I couldn't care less about when I'm sober. Like, I can hear a song from my childhood that I never really liked before and end up sobbing my heart out. It's embarrassing, but I can't help myself, and I drink more to help me feel better and can end up putting myself in risky situations. I know I'd be better without it.

I've tried to stop drinking so often. I would swear to give up for good, but I never got past a week. What would happen is that after a few days I would get this idea in my head that it will be different next time – it never is, but I fall for that idea every time.

I have read loads of books about stopping drinking and followed various blogs, but I just kept seeing the same advice that hadn't worked for me. Then I saw a post from Lewis that was a game-changer. He said I should stop thinking of sobriety as some boring and unhappy place (which I admit is how I did think) and look upon it instead as a being like a warm, protective blanket I could wrap around me anytime I needed it. I'd never heard that before, and I realized he was right because it was only when I was drinking that my life became miserable. When I was sober, life was okay and not much went wrong. I realized I'd been looking at drinking and sobriety back-to-front all my life!

That concept of the warm blanket was so powerful for me that I could go out with my drinking friends without being tempted to drink myself. I just visualized myself safe and snug in the blanket. Instead of being jealous that my friends could drink, I felt a bit sorry for them, like they were out there in a cold place.

I think I've also cracked something else that was holding me back. I think that I was making life hard for myself by saying I would give up for good. I'm only 30. Saying for good is too much. But I've learned the idea of taking a target that I knew I could manage and then just doing it again. So, I don't think about where I'm going in the distant *future, I just think about my next target. If I get the urge to drink, which I still do a lot, I just defer it in my mind until after my next target is done. You could say I kick the urge down the road, and when I get to it again, I just give it another kick down the road.*

I don't know how long that road is, but I don't need to know. What I do know is that I've never been four months sober before in my adult life. It's different this time. I've had the mind shifts, and my whole way of thinking about alcohol has changed forever. It's the sort of thing that once you know it, you can't unknow it again."

Day Nine.

The Alcohol FAQs.

Feedback from readers helped shape the content of this book. This chapter is no exception. The following FAQs all come from the subscribers to my email service. The subscribers are mostly people who have had issues with alcohol, but some are concerned relatives of drinkers or healthcare professionals. The one thing they have in common is that they have all read my writing.

I prefer to use email rather than social media because it's private and, in the interests of reader confidentiality, I prioritize privacy. (You can join my email service at subscribepage.com/emailservice.)

So, in no particular order, here are my readers' questions and my responses.

Question: *"Can a person give up alcohol without professional help? I ask as I have read lots of books but cannot stop drinking even though I know it cannot be healthy."*

My answer is a qualified yes. Research from the American Government's agency the NIAAA shows that the majority of people who have diagnosable alcohol problems overcome their difficulties without having any sort of treatment. But they tend to be younger people who lose interest in alcohol as they start careers, have families and so on. It's a process known as maturing out. The average age of onset is around 22 years old and lasts four years, although some people can have repeated episodes.

However, if you have gone past that stage, and if you have been trying to give up alcohol on your own for some years and can't make any progress, it might be time to get some professional help. Your doctor would be the logical person to go and see, or a qualified counsellor who specialises in addiction issues. It might be that a professional can see something that you can't see yourself.

Also, you should consider if you need some sort of social support. Stopping drinking on your own is hard. But it might be that if you enlist the support of family or friends, that might be all you need to encourage you to quit.

Question from a doctor: *"I've had several clients struggle with the choice of what to drink rather than alcohol, both at home and when eating out. They have concerns about the calories in sodas and if sweeteners in diet drinks are good for you. If you don't want caffeine,* *sodas, don't like iced tea, what's left? What's fun or interesting to drink that's not alcoholic and not loaded with calories?"*

My answer: In my experience, if someone is worrying about the calories in soda (which are fewer than alcohol) or the taste of certain drinks, it's just a smokescreen to mask wavering motivation. It usually means they are looking for an excuse to continue drinking. If they are really committed to reducing or quitting, they will find a suitable alternative to drinking.

Having said that, I think the most popular drinks among non-drinkers I know are tea, coffee, ginger beer and sparkling water. I wouldn't recommend alcohol-free beer or wine, as these are just one step away from the real thing.

Question: *"Why do you think it is that the harm alcohol can do to our health is not more widely known, particularly eye health? I have changes at 52 which could damage my sight. It's taken some time to be told it can be related to alcohol use."*

My answer: Alcohol's effects on eyesight aren't widely reported. Presumably, it isn't considered newsworthy enough. However, alcohol affects the eyes as it does every organ in the body. This may be at least in part due to vitamins being depleted as a result of alcohol in the bloodstream, and in particular lack of vitamin B1 (which we have already mentioned in this book concerning brain health) causing weakness of the eye muscles. Damage can be permanent.

However, I have found some anecdotal evidence in my work that eye damage can be reversed. I had one client whose distance eyesight had deteriorated to such an extent that he had stopped driving at night because he thought he was unsafe, even with glasses. He assumed the deterioration was due to middle age. But then he gave up drinking, and after a few months of sobriety, his eyesight improved so much that he didn't need distance glasses at all, even at night. There was no other logical explanation for the improvement. This was eight years ago, and he hasn't needed distance glasses since.

Question from a concerned relative: *"What can I do to help my sibling realize he needs to change and needs help to do it? It is so hard to bring up the topic when he is sober because he is so functional when he's not drinking. Our relationship with our father was always strained due to my dad's drinking. And my dad died of cirrhosis of the liver (69 yrs old)."*

My answer: I can see this is a situation that needs handling with care, as if he feels he is being confronted, he would be likely to become defensive and more entrenched in his behaviour.

Try to appear that you are on his side. Praise him for how he is when he's sober. You could say that you've done some research because you care about him, and the US Department of Health says that people with a family history of liver disease are at higher risk themselves. Say it would put your mind at ease if he had a liver function test to make sure he's OK. This would at least alert him to the risk and might prompt him to cut back or take longer breaks between spells of drinking.

Question: *"In your books, you often talk about therapy groups you run. They sound really good. How do they work, exactly? Where can I attend one, or one like yours?"*

My answer: The groups I have run have been when I have been working in public health in England, but you can find similar groups all over the world. My ones have been in an outpatient wing of a hospital, or in healthcare centres, or even a few in church halls. They usually last about an hour and a half and are discussion-based. I like to guide the discussion, not dominate it – no one wants to hear me drone

185

on for 90 minutes. I like to get about 8-12 people. Too few, and it can be a bit slow, but you don't want too many, so that everyone can get a chance to speak if they want.

There are different formats. Some meetings I run for drinkers only, but others will be for anyone with an issue around addictive behaviours. Some people are cross-addicted, the most common being alcohol and nicotine, which is a massively challenging combination – I call them the terrible twins. But sometimes you might get someone who is, say, cross-addicted to painkillers and gambling, which can liven things up.

Sometimes, I will have a theme ready-prepared for the group. But my favourite format, and the most informal, is to start with a check-in, which means that everyone can say a little about what's on their mind, and from that we draw up an agenda for discussion based on what the people in the room most want to talk about that day. Doing that, we don't go down the rabbit hole of what I think is important because it's what the group thinks is important that counts. We finish up with a quick check-out, where anyone can have a final say, and then get the coffee pot on.

That kind of format is the sort used for Smart Recovery meetings, and I have facilitated many Smart meetings.

Smart is a charity that started in the States and is strong in North America. In the UK, the public health service likes Smart, so you often find that local support agencies run Smart meetings. I believe they also have a good presence in Scandinavia and Australia.

One thing I like about Smart is that all their facilitators (which is what they call the people who run the meetings) are Smart-trained, so you get a consistency of message and a reliable standard wherever you go. I have done the Smart training twice, once for the UK and once for the USA, so I can vouch for its quality.

If you would like to try Smart but can't get to a meeting, or if you would like to put a toe in the water, you can try online meetings, which they regularly run out of the USA and the UK. Best place to start is SmartRecovery.org or SmartRecovery.org.uk.

Question: *"I'm not an alcoholic (I think) but when I drink heaviest, I adopt a self-destruct type attitude. I generally only drink on a Friday, Saturday, and Sunday, but when I'm feeling sad or down, it may creep into Thursday or even Wednesday. When I'm on holiday, I drink every night. I had cut down lots, but now some time has passed, and I'm back to bad habits."*

My answer: As you've cut down but then gone back to previous levels, it sounds like a break from drinking for a little while might help. It doesn't have to be forever – just enough time to reset your relationship with alcohol. You might find it easier to drink in moderation after that.

But long term, getting a different way of coping with emotional situations will help massively. It's a widely held belief that alcohol can help with low moods, but scientific research into the subject shows the exact opposite – it makes low moods even worse.

Question: *"I just can't beat the cravings. I'm 46 and have been dependant on alcohol for about 25 years. I work abroad on vessels for around 6 to 8 weeks at a time. There is no issue at work because alcohol is out of the picture as it's just not available. I have no cravings whatsoever. It's only when I know I can get hold of it. When I'm home, every day around midday time the craving comes, and I give in and go and get a beer – 8 to 12 cans of lager every day. I really need help to fight these cravings. I've read many books on alcohol problems, but your book seemed to strike a chord with me and made me understand many of the symptoms you talk about."*

My answer: You can't be physically dependent, or you would have a big physical reaction when you went back to work. It sounds like you have a deeply ingrained habit. Think of it as being like a computer program in your head, but the program only runs when you are at home. It might feel like physical cravings, but that's your mind playing tricks, although it feels very real.

The question is, what is the trigger that makes the program run? What's going on at home in the morning? Or is the problem something that's *not* going on, namely work, and you need to replace that? If you can work out what the trigger is, you can put a strategy in place to change your routine.

Question: *"I would love to stop drinking altogether, but as I drink a lot every day, I think I need to reduce first. My problem is, though, that I find reducing so hard, even if I drink one beer less a day, I feel it. Every time I try to reduce, it ends in a binge. Is there any medication I can get to help me cut down?"*

My answer: There are two medications. Naltrexone is a generic drug that has been around for many years and is used for other applications as well as alcohol reduction. Nalmefene is a newer drug, intended for drinkers, that is marketed by a drug company called Lundbeck under the name Selincro. These drugs cut down the desire to continue drinking once you have started. I have had several clients who have used these successfully to cut down. You would need to check with your doctor to see if either of these is licenced in your part of the world and if one of them would be suitable for you. There is a chapter in "Alcohol and You" that discusses medications for drinkers in more detail.

Question: *"Help!! I was six days into my detox, but I picked up a drink yesterday. I don't know how it happened. I usually drink at home with my partner. I was just chatting to her in the kitchen when I got in from work last night, and I suddenly realized I had a glass of wine in my hand. I must have gone into remote mode when I got home. She was having a drink as she isn't detoxing. I poured myself a glass of wine without realizing what I was doing. I had already taken a sip before I remembered I'm off the booze! I drank the glass but then put the bottle away. Have I blown it? Do I need to start again?"*

My answer: Technically speaking, you've broken your detox. But after six days, one glass isn't going to make much difference to what's happening in your body. Starting again from day one would seem like an over-reaction. Had you carried on drinking and had, say, a whole bottle, that would have been a different matter. Then it would have been a case of going back to day one.

I think what is more of a concern than the effect of one glass on your body is the effect on your mind. It could be that your subconscious is starting to undermine you. It might start telling you that if you have got away with it once, you can do it again. Before you know it, you'll be sliding down the slippery slope and all the good work you have done detoxing so far will be for nothing.

If you have the urge to drink again, try using the "Okay but not today" strategy to refocus on your target and tell your subconscious that this is really important to you and to support you rather than trying to trick you with thought bombs. I think it would be a good idea also to speak to your partner, make sure she knows what your target is, and ask her to support you. Drinking in front of you can't help you.

Question: *"I have been trying to stop drinking for a year, but I don't have any support and I just can't seem to do it on my own. I think I need support, but I don't want to go to my doctor as I don't want to have an alcohol problem on my health record. So I have been thinking about attending an AA meeting for the first time. I have looked online, and they seem to have meetings everywhere. But I hear they* *talk about God a lot and I'm not religious. And I heard they are like a cult. Also, they call themselves alcoholics and I don't think I'm an alcoholic – I'm not that bad. And I'm worried I might run into someone who knows me. What's your opinion? Should I give them a try?"*

My answer: Although I don't agree with AA on some things, I do have a lot of respect for them. They are, after all, the biggest recovery group in the world. However, the reservations you brought up are very common concerns. There's no getting away from the fact that you're going to hear the word God at an AA meeting. AA says they are spiritual rather than religious, but even that is too woo-woo for a lot of people (although some people like a bit of spirituality). It's the key thing that divides opinion about AA. In treatment circles you find people tend to be either very pro or very anti-AA – not many sit on the fence. But I must admit to being a fence-sitter myself.

AA certainly has its own way of doing things: it has a lot of rituals, and people can be very upset if you don't follow its etiquette. This can make it seem like a cult. But if it is a cult, it is at least a benevolent one. Some people love it and go to several meetings a week even though they have been sober for multiple years

I think the best thing to do is to go along to a meeting and decide for yourself. If you are worried about someone you know seeing you, then you could go to a meeting out of your area. But if someone you know is at a meeting, then they are there for the same reason as you. You need to be aware that AA has two types of meetings: open and closed. Anyone can attend an open meeting – you can just turn up and observe – but most meetings are closed, which means that only people who want to stop drinking are allowed. So if you go to a closed meeting, you are implicitly saying that you have an alcohol issue, even if you don't speak. But don't get concerned about whether you are an alcoholic. AA states that the only requirement for membership is that you have a desire to stop drinking, so you don't have to say you're an alcoholic. In fact, you don't have to say anything, which is probably a good idea at your first meeting.

My biggest worry about AA is its system of sponsors. A sponsor is a kind of mentor, and most people who have been in AA for more than a few weeks will have one. New members can be very reliant on their sponsors. As a treatment professional, I'm concerned that these people have no formal training – they are just AA members who have been sober for a while. A sponsor doesn't have to get a qualification or pass an interview, and as AA is an anonymous organization, they don't have to get a police check or even prove who they are. New members are often vulnerable, and this lack of sponsor-vetting or training doesn't sit well with me. There are some great sponsors, but I'm certain there are some terrible ones also.

You might not want to see your doctor because you are concerned about having alcohol on your medical record. But is that really a valid reason for not getting professional help? If you went to AA and liked it, you can be a member and get professional support at the same time – you don't have to choose between the two.

Question: *"I really struggle with cravings when I try to stop drinking. I've read up on triggers and ways of dealing with them and so on. But I just get really strong cravings in my body. Is there anything I can take that can help me? There are various herbal remedies on the internet, but they seem to be a waste of time."*

My answer: I'm not fond of using a drug to replace a drug, like taking medication to replace alcohol, but sometimes it can be helpful if all else fails. You might ask your doctor if acamprosate would be suitable for you. It's a drug that helps alleviate cravings. You can take it for a number of weeks after stopping drinking. It is, however, only suitable if you are planning to quit for the long term. It's not intended as a

194

stop-gap for someone just taking a short break from alcohol. Also, it's not a magic bullet. You would still need to use psychological tools as well.

Question: "I don't want to give up drinking. But I'm drinking every day and I'm concerned that I might be becoming dependent, even though I hold down a good job and look after my family. I have read, though, that some people can drink a lot without becoming dependent. What are the warning signs I should look out for?"

My answer: Here are some common signs to look out for:

- You find that you structure your day around when you can get a drink.
- You avoid going anywhere you need to drive in the evenings in order to drink.
- You won't go to restaurants that don't serve alcohol.
- You find it harder to stop in the evening and continue drinking later when you haven't got to work the following day.
- You start drinking earlier on non-workdays.
- You find that you need to drink more this year than you drank last year to reach the same level of intoxication.

- The time you take your first drink in the day is getting earlier.
- Your non-drinking days are becoming fewer.
- You have arguments with your partner about your drinking.
- You have problems at work because hangovers are affecting your performance.
- You continue drinking despite a medical warning.
- You find you can't pay off your credit card because you have run up a big bar bill on it.
- You have legal problems due to alcohol.

For me, the big red flag is if you find that you continue drinking even though you can see it's causing you serious problems.

Question: *"I don't want to stop drinking forever, but I intend to take your advice and have a complete break for a while. When I do drink again, I only want to be a moderate drinker. But what exactly is a moderate drinker? Is there a definition?"*

My answer: It's hard to give an exact definition in a book like this as it will be read internationally and advice varies from country to country. If you live in the United States, which is where this book is likely to be most widely read, there is a measure called a standard drink, which is equal to 0.6 ounces of alcohol. This means that a 12-ounce beer (5%) would be a standard drink. 5 ounces of wine (12%) would also be a standard drink, as would a 1.5 ounce shot of any 40% spirit, like vodka or whiskey. You are advised to only drink 2 standard drinks a day if you are a man and one if you are a woman, and not drink every day.

In the United Kingdom, where this book is also likely to be widely read, there is a different system called units. The easiest way to keep track of units is to read the bottle, can, or drinks menu because units must be shown by law. The daily limit is 3 units for men and 2 units for women, and you would be expected to have a couple of days off weekly.

When you consider that a pint of beer or an average glass of wine is 2 units or more, depending on the strength, you can see this daily limit isn't a lot if you've been used to drinking heavily. A binge is defined as 8 units in a day, but many people reading this book would think of that as normal. Because of this, a lot of drinkers who want to stay safe find it easier to stop completely, since drinking 2 or 3 units just gives them the taste for more rather than satisfying the desire to drink.

Another way to work out if you are drinking moderately is to use the Audit questionnaire in this book.

Day Ten.

Sobriety and Happiness.

We have touched already on the role of dopamine in forming habits. In this chapter, I will take this a step further to explain how having a little understanding of the way this works can help not only with staying sober but also being happier generally.

Dopamine is a neurotransmitter, a chemical messenger in your brain. When you are forming new habits, your brain releases dopamine to reinforce the new behaviour. As dopamine makes you feel good, you want to repeat the action to get another burst of it, and so the habit gets formed.

That's all well and good with a positive habit, such as getting yourself up and ready to do a good day at work. But the process of forming habits works equally well with creating bad habits. This is why unwanted habits can be so difficult to break: it's not just a question of changing your behaviour, you have to give up that dopamine hit as well, which goes against your natural instinct.

When habits become so hardwired in our behaviour that we feel we need them to exist, we often use another term:

addiction. Most people don't like the term addiction, as it gets used in a judgmental way. Even hard drug users, who know they have a serious addiction, tend to refer to their "habit". But whether you call them habits or addictions, we humans all have them, lots of them, and the range of things we can get addicted to is vast. Name anything, and there is probably someone somewhere who is addicted to it.

Something most of us experience at some point in our lives is being addicted to another person. Every time we see that person, we feel happier because we are getting a little dopamine spike, which continually reinforces the habit of wanting to be with that person. This kind of addiction is so common that it has a special name: love.

Most habits are behaviour-based, including potentially damaging addictive habits like gambling, watching excessive television, hoarding, porn, obsessive shopping, and video games. The internet and smartphones have produced a whole new crop of addictive behaviours. Have you ever found yourself randomly swiping your phone and realized you don't know why you're doing it? Yes, me too. The common link with all these behaviours is that we are looking for that feel-good dopamine hit, whether we get it from betting on football games or checking our Facebook posts for likes or whatever.

Certain substances produce a spike in dopamine. These vary from drugs to processed foods. The combination of habitual behaviours with substances is complex as it's not just the substance, but the ritual as well. Taking recreational drugs is ritualistic, as anyone who has ever passed a spliff will know. But so is eating fast food. If you are addicted to the complex mix of fats, sugars, salts, spices and additives in burgers, you are going to get bursts of dopamine from the moment you see the illuminated sign for your favourite eatery on the highway. Have you ever wondered why chain restaurants have the same format around the world? The combination of substances, habit and ritual is a compelling mix, and going into a restaurant that looks and functions the same in San Francisco as in Singapore plays on your desire for ritual. If eating spinach at home produced the same dopamine spike as eating cheeseburgers in a familiar restaurant layout, we wouldn't have an obesity problem in our society.

Profit is behind so much of this. Food companies spend stupendous amounts on experimenting with different combinations of edible substances to turn our taste buds into cash generators. Inventing one new type of chocolate bar can add billions to a company's bottom line for decades. That's not so different from how drug cartels developed crack to make cocaine even more habit-forming and profitable than it already was. You create the addict, then supply the demand. It's a proven way of making mega-money.

With alcohol, you have a heady combination of dopamine, sedation, intoxication, social indoctrination, big-money advertising, sparkling drinking places, enticing packaging, brand loyalty, tradition, socializing, and aggressive retailing to contend with. Small wonder drinking has become such a part of our culture.

All of those things are pushing your buttons to take a drink. Because of this, I have steered you towards replacing drinking with activities (the MAPs) that are pleasurable to you personally. If you try to replace all that with self-discipline, you are setting yourself up to fail because you are working against your own brain chemistry, as denying yourself a drink using willpower also means denying yourself those feel-good neurotransmitters. Whereas if you replace drinking with enjoyable projects, you will still be getting your dopamine and engaging in habits and rituals that are fun.

As an example, let's say you used to play the guitar, and you decide to take it up again as a Meaningfully Absorbing Project while you are having a sober break. As you rediscover old skills, listen to favourite albums you haven't heard for a while, and browse YouTube for videos of tutorials of music from legendary guitarists, your brain will be producing wave after wave of good feelings. You are using your brain chemistry to help you. If you are feeling good, why spoil it with drinking alcohol which is mood-altering, when your brain is producing pleasurable feelings for free?

Dopamine is not the only neurotransmitter. Serotonin is another, and it has an advantage over dopamine in that it lasts longer. Dopamine is a quick hit, which is why it is associated with addictions – as soon as it wears off, you are looking for the next dopamine high. You won't be consciously thinking of getting dopamine. You will be thinking of getting a beer, buying a pizza, watching the next episode of a box set, or whatever it is that's giving you those nice feelings at the time. Serotonin also feels good, but it isn't short-term and addictive like dopamine. It gives a longer-lasting feeling of happiness. Indeed, there's an argument for saying that serotonin actually *is* happiness.

Serotonin is associated with positive moods, social behaviour, good appetite, digestion, sleep, and sexual desire. Lack of serotonin, however, is associated with anxiety, poor sleeping patterns, low self-esteem, and even depression. In fact, the most common drugs for treating low mood and depression are called *Selective Serotonin Reuptake Inhibitors*, SSRIs, which work by boosting your serotonin levels. These include well-known drugs such as Citalopram, Fluoxetine, Sertraline and Prozac.

But you don't need to take a drug to boost your serotonin and your happiness. There are simple actions you can take that will achieve the same result.

Getting enough natural daylight is important. It's no coincidence that people are more likely to suffer from low mood and depression in the winter. So, making the most of the available daylight is the place to start.

Exercise is a big serotonin booster. As a bonus, exercise also releases another neurotransmitter, endorphins, which are like natural morphine – they help reduce pain and also prevent anxiety. That's why there is a chapter on movement in this book.

Relaxation, meditation and getting enough sleep will all increase your serotonin levels. You will find the relaxation exercise and the Flow Practice you have read about in this book helpful in this respect.

Sociability is great for serotonin production. So it's not a good idea to isolate yourself during your detox. If your social life usually revolves around alcohol, look at ways you can use your Meaningfully Absorbing Projects to generate new social activities that don't involve having a drink. One thing that will help in a big way is considering how you can contribute to your family or social group because serotonin comes from giving activities rather than taking.

To illustrate the difference between dopamine and serotonin, consider this: if you like chocolate, you will get a nice dopamine buzz if someone gives you a piece of chocolate cake. But it's a taking activity and the buzz will be short-term. On the other hand, if you bake a chocolate cake and give it away to your friends, that's a giving activity, and the feeling of wellbeing that the serotonin generates will last a long time. You will experience it as soon as you start work on the cake, while you are giving it to your friends, and for a while later you will continue to feel good about yourself.

The clients I work with are usually self-absorbed. I encourage them to look outwards and think about how they can focus their attention on giving to other people. That gets their brain chemistry working, cranks up the serotonin, makes them feel good, and makes them popular with their families and friends. Consequently, getting sober becomes a fun activity, not the doom and gloom that some think – those people who haven't yet made the mind shift.

A New Vision for You.

Congratulations! You have reached Day 10!

You have covered a lot of ground in this book and, I hope, learned some wonderful strategies that will help you keep the upper hand on alcohol for the rest of your life.

Today is a great time to reflect on the journey you have taken over the last 10 days and look ahead to where you go next.

Early in this book, I invited you to take a mind shift and look upon sobriety as a place of safety, comfort, and ease where you can go any time when life is getting challenging, or just when you want to feel cosy and secure. Life is much easier when you have eliminated the risk of DUIs, saved a ton of money, and been able to wake up in the morning in the happy knowledge that you haven't done anything crazy that you can't remember.

You should be feeling physically well and mentally focused. Your body and mind have started the work of restoring you to the condition of a non-drinker. And with every day you stay sober, your head will become clearer, your eyesight better, your immune system stronger, your weight easier to manage, your thinking quicker, and the risk of serious illness will recede. You have started to find peace of mind.

You have learned the importance of having a clear target, so what is your target today? If it was just to reach 10 days, I would suggest you consider extending your stay in the comfort and ease of sobriety. You have just done the hard work of going through the detox period, so why not stick around a bit longer and enjoy the benefits? After all, if you had just climbed a mountain, would you want to begin the descent immediately, or would you want to stay for a while, admire the view, savour the moment, and revel in the feeling of achievement?

Take a moment to review your target today. Now that you have a sober head, you might find that your target needs revising. Remember it's vital to have a target that you know you can achieve, and today you know for certain that you can manage 10 days.

Is your target realistic? Or is it too long and you need to break it down into smaller chunks? Or is it too easy and you need to extend it? You will know when you have the right target because it will motivate you. You should be able to look at your target and think, "Yes, I know I've got this."

You have all the tools you need to reach your target. You have learned about thought bombs and how to diffuse them, reprogramming your subconscious to support you, and how to relax without alcohol. You've discovered how to navigate safely around the triggers of people, places, times and events. You have explored the power and pleasure of having a Meaningfully Absorbing Project that takes your mind into a rewarding place where intoxication is unwanted.

You have taken a critical look at your true motivation and learned how the simple tactic of keeping the score can spur you on. You have seen how the ingrained patterns of habits and rituals run your life, but you can turn them to your advantage. You have discovered that when life all gets too much and your mind is scattered, you can turn to the tranquillity of the Flow Practice to keep you safe. You have explored some of the darker sides of your feelings and how movement can set you free.

A reader wrote a review of one of my other books on Amazon the other day. In it, she wrote, "This book is about so much more than just alcohol." If you have taken the time to absorb the ideas and strategies in the book you are holding now, you might have realized that this book is also about much more than alcohol. You have learned skills that can transform your life, not just your drinking.

211

An old book about drinking finished with a chapter called "A Vision for You", in which it described what the future could be like for a sober person. But I have faith in you that you can do even better. I have faith that you can manage without an off-the-peg future and instead create a vision of your future, bespoke and unique to you.

I invite you to create this vision today.

What Next? An Update.

Since I wrote the book you have just read, the 10-Day Alcohol Detox Plan has helped many thousands of people, succeeding beyond my expectations.

I have received positive feedback from countless of readers in that time. However, one request has come up time and again: many readers want a follow-up book to give them long-term structure and support.

I have now created that book – *Mindfulness for Alcohol Recovery: Making Peace with Drinking.*

Mindfulness is the basis of much of what you have learned in the 10-Day Alcohol Detox Plan. In fact, I believe that mindfulness is the most important treatment for alcohol issues of the 21st century. If you want a more advanced book to follow on from the 10-day program, Mindfulness for Alcohol Recovery is ideal.

You can see all my books on my website WinsPress.com, and on your local Amazon site.

I Need Your Help!

That brings us to the end of the main part of "The 10-Day Alcohol Detox Plan". But before you go on to read the bonus pages, I have a small favour to ask.

If you have found this book helpful, we would be massively grateful if you could leave a review on Amazon. Reviews are so important to a new book. The more reviews I get, the more likely Amazon will promote this book and put it in the hands of people who need it.

It's easy to do in 3 simple steps:

1. Use the following link, which is a shortcut to go to the book's page on Amazon: viewbook.at/10-day-detox
2. When you get to the book's page, scroll down to near the bottom, and click on the button on the left which says, "Leave a customer review".
3. Give it a star rating, add any comments you want other readers to see, and the job is done!

Thank you so much for doing a review.

Appendix.
How to Find the Right Direction for You.

Targets are one of the essential tools discussed in this book. I wrote in the "Targets and Rituals" chapter that I would include an appendix that will help anyone who struggles to work out targets that are right for them.

The following few pages are an extract from my book "Change Your Life Today" which I think will help you this is a problem for you.

"Change Your Life Today" was written for anyone, not just drinkers. But anyone can suffer from indecision sometimes, so I hope the following pages help.

It All Begins with Desire.

Have you ever wanted something, only to find out when you got it, that it failed to do for you what you thought it would?

Maybe you wanted a certain kind of relationship, but when you found it, you still felt unfulfilled. Perhaps it was a dream job, but when you got it, you found it unsatisfying and you wanted to do something else. Maybe you wanted a possession that you thought would make you feel happy, but by the time you got it, your mind had already moved on to the next thing you thought would make you feel better. Perhaps you heard of a drug that you thought might transform how you felt, but after you took it, life just seemed even worse. Maybe you wanted to live in a certain place, only to discover that when you moved there, you still felt empty inside.

If something like this has happened to you, then in all probability the reason was that what you thought you wanted was unaligned with your deep-down desires. So, when you got what you thought you wanted, it didn't light up your life as you thought it would. Instead, it was a disappointment because your underlying desire was still unmet.

Or have you ever thought that you wanted something, but just somehow couldn't muster the motivation to go after it? You tried to use motivational techniques but procrastinated anyway. You maybe even thought there was something wrong with you, that you were lacking in some way.

If this has happened, then it's likely that the same lack of alignment was the problem. You couldn't get the motivation to go for your goal, because, deep down inside of you, on an unconscious level, you knew it wouldn't meet your true desire.

This lack of alignment is an easy trap to fall into. It happens all the time. It has certainly happened to me. A common reason for this is that what we think we want is, in fact, what someone else wants. We are doing something to please other people. Or it may be that what you think you want is because of social conditioning: you are doing what you think society expects. You do things because that's the way it's always been done, without questioning if it's the right way for you.

People do things because they think they *should* do something. For instance, my wife once thought she *should* do a law degree. It seemed to make sense, as it was a good degree to have. But it wasn't her desire, her heart wasn't in it. After a year she abandoned it and studied history instead, which she enjoyed, and got that degree.

Some years ago, I thought I *should* get into IT work as the money seemed good, so I set up a business designing bespoke databases. The business made money right away. But I had to give it up after a year because I became very unhappy in the work. It simply wasn't my desire at all. I really couldn't have cared less about databases – I was just doing it for the money, which rarely works out well in the long-term.

If that word *"should"* is involved, you can be pretty sure you are doing something that is unaligned with your true desire.

This can have disastrous outcomes. For example:

- People end up in the wrong career because they are trying to fulfil their parents' ambitions for them, rather doing what would bring them joy and deep satisfaction.
- Some find themselves trapped in unhappy marriages because they think that they need a partner who fits certain stereotypes, rather than someone they truly love.

- Others live a lifestyle which is not natural for them and brings them unhappiness because they are afraid of stepping outside the social norms they were brought up with.
- Some lose unhealthy amounts of weight, or even get surgery, trying to look like the models in airbrushed images they see in magazines, tragically not realizing that they looked great all along.
- Still others turn to prescription or illicit drugs and, in the end, find they need to keep taking them just to feel normal.

So, before you begin the task of changing your life for the better, you need to know from the outset that your goal is aligned with your deep-down desire, otherwise, disappointment or worse will surely follow. Achieving a goal that you never truly desired will sap your energy and resources and just leave you feeling empty, or perhaps even desperate.

However, you can use a simple technique to test your goal and check that it really is your true desire. I call it the *"Why is that?"* strategy. I have used this successfully with many of my therapy clients and I also use it on myself regularly. I suggest you use it yourself before you get deeper into this book. This is how it works.

Ask yourself, what do you want? Then ask yourself, why is that? When you have the answer, ask again, why is that? Keep asking the question for each answer you come up with, until you are sure you have drilled right down to your deepest desire.

I will illustrate how this works with a real-life example. I had a new client called Sam come to see me. Sam was a 27-year old self-employed builder, who lived with his wife and their young child. Things were going well. He was happy in his relationship. They lived in a fine apartment that Sam had lovingly refurbished himself. He had all the work he needed – the money was pouring in and he had taken on staff. There was, however, one big snag. Sam was spending all his spare income on his cocaine habit. He had come to me for counselling.

With this type of problem, the counsellor will usually try to help the client to focus on a positive activity to replace their addiction. So, when I initially spoke to Sam, I asked him to think about what he really wanted, then tell me what it was when we next met. This is what happened:

"So, Sam, have you chosen a positive goal for yourself?" I asked at the start of our next meeting.

Sam nodded and said: "I want to buy one of the white houses by the park." I knew the houses he meant. They were imposing, expensive and much bigger than Sam needed for his small family.

"Really? I thought you loved your apartment."

"I do," Sam replied. "But I want to move."

"Why is that?" I asked.

"It would be great to have a big place when my relatives come to visit," he said. "We have a family get-together at my place a couple of times a year. It would really impress them."

"You want a bigger house to impress your relatives? Why is that?"

"Well," he hesitated, "it's just that sometimes I think they look down on me."

"Really? Why is that?"

Sam started to open up: "My brother Darren was always the bright one in our family. He was the one who got a university degree. He went into banking and is doing really well for himself. I guess if I got a house more like his, the family would see me more as his equal."

Now we were getting down to what Sam's real desire was. It wasn't the new house at all, he was happy in his apartment. What he really desired was to feel as valued as his brother.

"So," I responded, "what have people in your family said to make you think that they don't see you as equal?"

"Well, nothing really," he said, uncertainly. "But I guess with him being a banker and me a builder…"

I could see that the problem was not in the family's perception of Sam, but Sam's perception of his own status. Getting a bigger house was unlikely to change that. Over the next couple of sessions, we worked on Sam's feelings of self-worth. He was particularly helped by a technique I call *Achievement Stacking*, which I will be describing in a later chapter.

Sam began to see that what he had done as a builder was really to his credit, and the idea that his family looked down on him was an illusion of his own making. He turned his focus to expanding his business, which in turn built up his self-esteem, and his cocaine habit faded as it became irrelevant to his life.

You can see from Sam's story how simple but powerful the "Why is that?" strategy is. It really can be a revelation to people when they realize what they truly desire. In my exchange with Sam, I used "Why is that?" three times, and very quickly I was able to uncover what Sam's true desire really was, which on a conscious level, Sam hadn't seen himself.

Sam didn't realize I was using a technique to help him. But you can use it in a very conscious way with yourself. Keep asking "Why is that?" until you get to the truth. You might surprise yourself, as your unconscious mind gives up a secret it had been hiding from your conscious mind.

You can also use it in a caring way to help people in your life. It works on all levels. You can use it with your spouse or your parents. Equally, you can use it with your children as part of your parenting skills. It is also invaluable with work colleagues. If you are in any kind of management role, it will help you understand your employees' needs. But conversely, you can use it with your own manager to better understand what your organization requires of you.

However, I will add a couple of caveats to this strategy. Firstly, if you use "Why is that?" to drill down to your true desire, and it shows you something dark, something that could hurt you or other people, such as a desire to harm yourself in some way, then please get professional help.

Secondly, if you use it with other people, do so in a helpful and compassionate way, rather than try to catch people out.

But what if you are still unclear about what you really want? Let's look at that next.

But I Don't Know What I Want.

Some people have found that using the "Why is that?" strategy doesn't work initially, because they can't answer the first "What do you want?" question. Most of the clients I have worked with in my professional life as a therapist have wanted change. But for many of them, they were constantly frustrated because they didn't know what the change was that they were looking for. They didn't know what they wanted – they just knew they wanted something better.

This can be a massive issue for people who pass from year to year without any sense of direction. They go around and around in circles in their minds, trying to find the answer. I have had clients in tears of frustration because they just can't decide what they want. Some people go through their entire lives in this miserable state.

I have come to realize that there can be different reasons why people find themselves in this situation. The first reason is being overwhelmed. This happens when so much needs fixing in someone's life that they are mind-blown about where to start and end up taking no action at all. They are bewildered about what to prioritize. Imagine having multiple fires burning in your life but having only one bucket of water. Which fire should you put out? What about the rest?

I've found this is usually the case with people I have counselled for self-destructive behaviour. Let's take excessive gambling as an example. They learn to stop the compulsion to gamble, but then find that they have to get on with dealing with the trouble the gambling had caused, like debts, broken relationships, lost housing, and ruptured careers. These clients often find they are frozen by indecision. They have ended their self-destructive behaviour, but they still have multiple fires burning in their lives.

Another situation might be where a client has already achieved a goal, and this has left them directionless. A common situation I have encountered, for example, is where someone has worked for years for retirement. This goal has kept them motivated and given their life meaning. Then the golden day comes when they can retire, and for a few weeks or months, it's wonderful – they can do what they like. But then they realize that they need a goal once more, but simply can't decide what. In the past, they didn't have to think about it. The goal was clear – retirement. Now they can't find anything which gives them that same compelling drive, and they miss that.

Other clients I have worked with have had their lives turned upside down by a sudden change in circumstances, such as unemployment, or relationship break-up, or a medical condition that has meant the person can no longer do what they used to. It leaves them feeling directionless and lost.

If you are one of those people waiting for that magical day when the clouds part and your true meaning is revealed to you like a blinding beam of sunlight, you might wait a long time. You might die waiting.

But there is a fix. In this chapter, I shall explain some different strategies that I have seen work for many clients. Look at these and see if there is one that can help you in your life.

Firstly, take a piece of paper and brainstorm with yourself (or maybe with the help of someone you trust) anything you might want to do. Don't worry about how crazy your ideas might be, just get writing. Make the longest list that you can. Keep going until you feel you have exhausted your mind of ideas.

Once you have done that, give each item on the list a score out of five for how *important* you think it is. Be careful that you are rating it as how important you think it is to *you*, not how important it is to someone else. Do you remember what we have already said about things you think you *should* do? Where that word *"should"* is involved, it usually means that you are doing something for someone else, or because of someone else's values. You are unlikely to get a good outcome because it will be someone else's desire, rather than yours.

Having done that, go through your list again and give each item another score out of five, this time for how *urgent* it is to you. Be careful to understand that important and urgent mean two quite different things. For example, if I want my car to work, I would give putting fuel in the tank five for importance. But if I already have a full tank, I would only give it one for urgency. If I had half a tank, I would give it maybe three for urgency. If the indicator was on the red and the engine was running on fumes, I would give it five for urgency. Just because something is important doesn't mean it's urgent, and vice-versa.

Now go through your list again and add your scores for importance and urgency together for each item. You now have a total score out of ten for each item. The item that has

230

the highest score out of ten would be a great place for you to be focusing your attention.

This system for prioritising works on many levels. It can be used to sort out major life priorities, or it works just as well for short term focusing, such as optimizing your work schedule. It's also useful if you have a particular project happening, such as starting a business or buying a property. You start with addressing the item with the highest score then work down the list in order of the score.

The feedback clients have given me for this system has always been positive. It really cuts through the confusion. As one client said to me, it gives "instant clarity."

Another system I have seen work well for people trying to get focus on the big issues in their lives is this: instead of asking yourself what you want, try asking yourself what you fear most.

We all have fears. The most successful person you know has fears. The most confident person you know has fears. Having rational fears is healthy; it keeps you safe from real dangers. Even irrational fears such as phobias can be quite harmless unless they are extreme.

So, what do you fear? What do you desire *not* to happen? Maybe loneliness, ill health, business failure, old age, disease, whatever it is, put it to the "Why is that?" test to see if there is more going on than you consciously realised.

When you have your answer, you can start turning your fear to your advantage. To do this, ask yourself what you could really do to take you as far as possible away from what you fear. For example, if your fear is being overwhelmed by financial worries, your aim might be to downsize your commitments. If you fear ill health, your aim might be to change your eating and activity habits. If you fear loneliness, your aim might be to join an organization where you will meet like-minded people. And so on.

Finally, another way to address the problem of lack of focus is to start by looking at what you're good at or have the potential to be good at. Everyone has some sort of talent. What's yours?

If nothing instantly springs to mind, think carefully, look at things you have done in the past that have gone okay, and get together a list. Maybe it could be something you have done before but stopped doing, or something you do now, but not in a committed way. Is there something that you could be focusing on that you could get really good at?

The theme of this book is about using change for success and happiness. If there is something that you can focus on and enjoy success with, happiness will usually follow. We all like the feeling of doing something well, whatever that is.

Using the ideas that you have read about so far, you should be able to find out what, for you personally, is your desire.

Thank You.

I hope you found that extract from "Change Your Life Today" helpful.

You can see all my books and read free extracts at WinsPress.com.

On the same site, I also post free articles and audios for you to enjoy and draw inspiration from. Check out what's available under the "Free Stuff" tab.

And remember to listen to the free podcast "The Alcohol Recovery Show", which can be found at winspress.com/podcast, and on most major podcast platforms.

Thank you for reading "The 10-Day Alcohol Detox Plan".

I wish you all the very best,

Lewis David.

Made in United States
North Haven, CT
06 October 2023

42428873R00134